How to start a successful Daycare business during COVID-19

*Helpful suggestions and ideas from a
Licensed/Registered Daycare Provider of 21 years
and mother of three.*

Whether you are just starting your Daycare
or have had one for years,
this Guide can help you start for the first time
or modify your current Daycare program.

By: **Tamara J. Hessler**

Copyright © 2020 Tamara J. Hessler All rights reserved

No part of this book may be reproduced, or stored in a retrieval system, or transmitted in any form or by any means, electronic, mechanical, photocopying, recording, or otherwise, without express written permission of the publisher.

ISBN: 9798587338555

Cover design by: Canva and Art Painter
Printed in the United States of America

Dedication

I would like to dedicate this book to my dear late friend Michael Welle, who a long time ago gave me the idea to write this book.

Also, to my daughter, Emily for her amazing support and help in organizing and editing.

Foreword

     I basically grew up in my mom's daycare which was run out of our home. As a child, I had these "automatic friends" to play with each day and then after school. As I grew up, I learned how to help care for the children whom I would later babysit as well.

     Growing up in a daycare teaches you many things. I learned tips and tricks to managing a household with many children. I learned how different parenting styles work and don't work, and what behaviors it yields in their children.

     I also grew to respect my mom as a business owner. She took her business very seriously and cared for those children like her own. She cared about their well-being, their academic growth, and their home life as well.

     I hope you will enjoy the process of running your daycare, modifying it, or simply learning the perspective of a daycare provider. Many hours and lots of love have gone into this book.

Emily A. Hessler, J.D.
Editor

Table of Contents

INTRODUCTION 1

CHAPTER 1: STARTING FROM GROUND ZERO 4
    LICENSE AND REGISTRATION PLEASE 4
    INSURANCE 7
    ADVERTISING FOR DAYCARE OPENINGS 8

CHAPTER 2: CONTRACTS 11
CONTRACT VIOLATIONS 13
    CONTRACT MODIFICATION 15

CHAPTER 3: PROGRAM AND POLICIES 17
    SICK POLICY 17
    PERMISSION FORMS 20
    IMMUNIZATIONS: 20

CHAPTER 4: RUNNING A DAYCARE DURING COVID-19 21

CHAPTER 5: RATES 23
    DON'T GET HUNG UP ON THE "PER HOUR" 25
    INFANT/BABY'S RATES 27
    SUDDEN INFANT DEATH SYNDROME (SIDS) 30

CHAPTER 6: HOURS OF OPERATION 31
    LATE PICKUPS 32
    BABYSITTER VS. DAYCARE PROVIDER 33
    FULL-TIME AND PART-TIME 34
    BABIES 34

CHAPTER 7: INTERVIEWING 35
    SPECIAL NEEDS 36
    TAKING FRIENDS/RELATIVES INTO YOUR DAYCARE 36

CHAPTER 8: TERMINATION 38
    A NOTE ON RECORDKEEPING 38

  DEALING WITH DIFFICULT PARENTS 39

CHAPTER 9: RECORDKEEPING 42

  KEEPING RECORDS ON CHILDREN 42

CHAPTER 10: PREPARING YOUR HOME FOR DAYCARE 45

  OUTSIDE 45
  PLAYSETS/SWING SETS 46
  SANDBOXES 46
  OUTDOOR TOYS 47
  BEING A COURTEOUS NEIGHBOR WHO WORKS FROM HOME 47
  INSIDE 48
  THE PLAYROOM 50
  TOYS 51
  AFTER-SCHOOL KIDS TOYS 51

CHAPTER 11: EQUIPMENT 52

  CRIBS FOR BABIES: 52
  MESHED SIDED PORTABLE CRIBS (PACK-N-PLAY) 52
  STROLLERS 53
  WALKERS/STATIONS 53
  INFANT TOYS 54
  INFANT/TODDLER AND PRESCHOOL CAR SEATS 54

CHAPTER 12: SAFETY 55

  CELL PHONES 55
  EMERGENCY CARDS 55
  T-SHIRTS 55

CHAPTER 13: SO... WHO PAYS FOR STUFF? 56

  DIAPERS 56
  PULL-UPS 56
  WET WIPES 56
  CLOTH DIAPERS 56
  SUNSCREEN 57
  STORAGE 57

  Baby's Milk/Formula 57
  Tissues 58

Chapter 14: To Provide or Not to Provide Food… 59
  Breakfast 59
  Lunch 59
  Food Programs 60

Chapter 15: Media 62

Chapter 16: A Family-Friendly Home 63
  Winter 64
  Summer 65
  The Playroom 66
  Pets/Animals 67

Chapter 17: Preschool Programs 68
  Schedule Routine 68
  Cleaning Routine 69
  Arts and Crafts 70
  Friday Folders 72

Chapter 18: Birthdays and Holidays 73
  Birthdays 73
  Tips and Tricks 73
  Christmas break 75
  Christmas/Holiday Party 76
  Working with Families on Vacations 80
  Religion in Daycare 81

Chapter 19: Maternity Leave 82

Chapter 20: Taxes 84
  Hours 85

Chapter 21: Your Own Kids in Daycare 87
  Needing Adult Interaction 88

Chapter 22: Making a Difference 91

CHECKLIST: SETTING UP THE HOME 94
CHECKLIST: PLAYROOM 95
CHECKLIST: FOR OUTSIDE PLAYGROUND 96
CHECKLIST: FOR OUTSIDE TOYS 97
SUPPLIES NEEDED FOR EVERYDAY 98
SUPPLIES TO BE BROUGHT BY FAMILIES 99
PROGRAM AND POLICIES FORM 100
ADMISSIONS CONTRACT FORM 110
SWIMMING PERMISSION FORM 113
TAX FORM FOR DAYCARE FAMILIES 114
RATES TEMPLATE 115
NOTE ON RATES: 116
FILE INFORMATION REQUEST FORM 117

Tamara J. Hessler

Introduction

We didn't expect to be home, and not working. But here we are, it's 2020 and COVID-19 has taken our jobs, and our livelihood. If you ever thought in the back of your mind to have your own business, this just might be the right one for you, during this time and beyond.

I never saw myself doing Daycare, yet there I was starting one out of my home. For the next 21 years, I was completely immersed in it. I grew up in Minnesota, in a moderately sized town, surrounded by beautiful farms, fields of corn, and beans. I was raised Catholic and my mother was a stay-at-home mother, but of course, in those days most mothers were. I am the fourth of five children and I wasn't too happy about my younger brother coming along and taking my position of "baby" when I was 6 years old. At least he was a boy so I could still keep my place as the youngest girl. I had a great group of girlfriends and we spent many days downtown, going to movies, window shopping, and stopping at the popular Broiler Cafe' for fries and cokes. Funny how most of us never talked about college or careers, I think most of us saw ourselves like our mothers, raising a family, living in our town and staying friends forever and of course our kids would be friends too, like us.

Well, we did remain friends forever, but most of them stayed in our little town to this day--though it has grown so much I barely can navigate around when I visit. A few of us continued after high school with college or tech school, but most married and raised their families while I moved away to Wisconsin. I married way too young and had my first child at the ripe age of barely twenty. I was sure I knew everything there was to know. When I look at the girls of age twenty now, I ask myself, "what was I thinking?!". But I had the most beautiful baby boy and was thrilled. My mother used to say to me, "you sure haven't slowed down a bit, you and your child sure get around". I would tell my son, "what a good little traveler you are" since there were many trips back to Minnesota to see family and friends. We would hit up McDonald's, grab a burger and fries to go, and turn the music on and we'd drive down I-90 through the hills of Wisconsin and on to the farmlands of home!

How to Run a Daycare

It's hard to believe that my little boy is now forty-three years old, married to his high school sweetheart with a son of his own. He is retired after twenty years in the Air Force. Time has gone by way too fast. It seems I was only in my twenties a few years ago. I find that I have my mother's youthful genes since people are always surprised to hear my age. I attribute my youthfulness to children! God's beautiful little ones... who will tell you they love you, write you impressive notes of admiration, and masterpieces of finger paint or color markers that clutter the fridge, but will also let you know that your gray hair is showing without hesitation. My youngest likes it when I wear a ponytail and a baseball cap, she says it makes me look younger. It's usually to cover my grey roots, but I do like the look of the cap.

So, life has changed a bit since the days in my hometown of Mankato, MN. I've married more than once. I have three beautiful children. I told you of my son, but I also have two girls, Emily Anne and Kelly Rose. Their dad and I divorced when they were ages 13 and 11. They kept busy, one being a cheerleader, the other in the dance team. Both would later join the high school marching band playing the flute and piccolo. They placed in the All-State band every year and my oldest, Emily, was Drum Major her senior year and Kelly was Section Leader of the Flutes.

I loved every moment of those years. Because I was working for myself, I was able to alter my schedule when I needed or wanted to. If they had a competition out of town, I would close early that day, with notice of course. It was nice to have some flexibility to be able to do things like that. I was also home when they came home from school or called because they forgot their flute or a book. I could load the kids into my daycare van and bring the forgotten item to school. While out, I would often take the daycare kids to the city park for some morning playtime.

There are many perks to being your own boss. But it takes a thorough plan and courage, support, and guidance. I am hoping while you read through this, you will highlight things and make notes that you want to be sure to remember. I hope you will take some relief from it as well. You are receiving some very good and helpful advice from an experienced Daycare provider. I had my next-door neighbor who did daycare and educated me through so much of my career in daycare. She supported me when I would call with frustrations, sometimes even through tears. By the time we were done talking I had a plan and things were better for it. I felt stronger and at times validated for my feelings. I am hoping this book will serve as your "next-door neighbor".

Whether you are just starting your Daycare or have had one for years, this Guide can help you start for the first time or modify your current Daycare. This book can also be used as a reference guide when things come up through the years, and *they will*…. I assure you.

So….let's get started!

Chapter 1: Starting from Ground Zero

The following information is taken from my own experience starting up a daycare and staying in business for over 21 years. I won't claim to have all the answers, but from trials to triumphs, I feel very qualified to help you get started, create a business you can be proud of, be a great and sought-after Daycare Provider, and help you be home and still contribute financially to your family's welfare. So, let's get down to some nitty-gritty business setup stuff you need to know before we get into the rest.

License and Registration Please

First, contact your local Department of Social Services to find out when and where classes or meetings will be conducted, and to begin the paper process of starting your Daycare Business to get registered or licensed. Some may not have a class or meeting and will simply send you a large packet of all the forms to be filed with the state.

Second, plan to be finger-printed. Anyone in the household who is over the age of 15 (in most states) and living in the home will need to be fingerprinted and have a background check done. Some states will do this on individuals as young as 13 or 14 as well. You may also need to have several personal references regarding your character. Be honest and answer everything to the best of your ability and the State will let you know if there is any problem with your information or background check. The State or County is looking for situations that could present a problem such as recent DUI's, Felonies, incidents involving children, parents behind in child support payments, etc.

Most states will allow Daycare for unlicensed and unregistered persons if only *one* family is in your care regardless of the number of children. For example, if you only care for the Smith family's 5 children, you could do so unlicensed and unregistered so long as it is only the Smith family in your care. Similarly, if you are only caring for relatives, a small number of children, or only for a few hours a day you may also be exempt from licensing. Your local DSS will be able to answer whether this is allowed in your area.

Some states will only have licensing available with a specific number of children allowed in the home, including your own. Other states will allow both licensed and registered daycare homes. A registered daycare allows fewer children than a licensed one, which has more strict inspections. Licensed homes must have windows in the bathrooms, while registered homes do not have to. Licensed homes get scheduled and surprise visits. Up until 2016, registered homes did not do home visits unless a complaint was made.

- Licensed homes are visited by the County DSS in which you reside for an inspection, at which time they will give you a list either at the inspection or send you a list of things you will need to address in your home to get it up and ready for daycare, and then will return to inspect again before you are allowed to start your daycare.
- The Fire Marshall will also visit and have a requirement list.
- You may also have a visit from the City, and they may require that you pay a nominal fee to have a business within your home. I had to pay $10 to my city in South Carolina.
    - An example of one of the criteria needed to be met is that all cars/vans need to have room within your driveway for picking up and dropping off, so you don't use the street, causing traffic issues.
    - They may also require you to have certain square footage in your home designated for your business. A licensed daycare will only be allowed on the first level of your home for all business conducted in some states.
    - Other states will allow, for example, a split-level home to use both levels provided that the lower-level windows are of normal size to allow for an exit if needed. Egress windows are legal as well. Windows will also be required in bathrooms and all sleeping rooms. However, my SC home had 2 bathrooms used for daycare and neither one had a window as they were located in the middle of the home.
    - Some states will require that all children nap within the same room, however, there seems to be an exception for babies that sleep in a crib in a different room, or if you have a child who won't leave the others alone to nap.

How to Run a Daycare

Your local DSS worker will make 1-2 scheduled visits with you each year, and at least one surprise visit. At this time, they will check on your number of children allowed within your license and will count heads. Records for each child will be checked and should have all the following:
1. Immunization records
2. Enrollment form with all pertinent information on parents and children.
3. They may check for extension cords and gates.
4. They may check your tag on your fire extinguisher to be sure it is up to date on inspection.
5. Your License should be posted in a prominent place
    a. I always had mine in a frame and on the wall near my front door.
6. Your Fire/Storm log to show your DSS Worker that lists what dates you had a fire drill or storm drill for every month.
    a. I kept my Fire/Storm drill sheet taped to the inside of my foyer closet door for quick access and not something unsightly in my home decor.

Something I did in my daycare in MN and in SC that was fun for the kids is I had them paint a fire blazing on a large piece of tagboard. We wrote the word "FIRE!!!" on it too. I told the children if they ever noticed it in any room within the house they were to yell "fire!" and now the fire drill would begin. We would end our drill at our designated meeting place, which for us, was the electric box on the front corner of our lot next to the sidewalk in front of our house. I always did the storm drill the same day the city had its siren test. We would hear the siren the first Wednesday of each month and that would signal us to start our storm drill and we would file into the laundry room or in the closet under the stairs.

Previously, a Registered Daycare would most likely not have a visit from either DSS or the City or even the Fire Marshall for checkups. However, in the last few years that I had my business (2015-2017), DSS was starting to make surprise visits due to some serious issues with some home daycares in the county. I was a Licensed Daycare provider for up to 12 children when I was in MN and I lived in a split-level home.

When I was in SC, I was a Registered Daycare because my home didn't meet the requirements of a Licensed Daycare, thus only 6 children were allowed. You do not need to count your own children if they are over the age of 10 or other children over the age of 10. Check with your local DSS as to what the exact age may be, as each county/state could be different. This can make a huge impact on how many kids you have in your care.

When each of my daughters turned 10, I didn't have to include them in my allowed daycare kids, thus being able to earn more money with more children. MN had stricter rules than SC, though I ran my SC daycare as I did in MN because it simply made sense. I wasn't required to have a flexible escape ladder when we lived in SC in case of fire, but why wouldn't I? It was for the safety of my own family and those in my daycare. I also wasn't required to have a fire extinguisher on the second level, but I did because my daycare was over the garage and the kids slept up there as well as my family. I kept it under the sink in the kid's bathroom upstairs along with the box with the ladder. **It is never wrong to be careful.**

When we bought our home in SC, I wasn't aware that I wouldn't qualify to be licensed since the two bathrooms used for daycare were in the middle of the house and thus had no windows so I only qualified to be registered. If you plan on buying or building, and you want to run a daycare, be sure you know what you need to have to be licensed. It makes a huge difference in income going from 12 kids to 6 kids.

Insurance

Check with your homeowner's insurance agent on a plan to cover your daycare in case of an accident or claim against you. It is a good idea, though I never did, to incorporate your daycare as a separate identity. Should you be sued, they could only go after your daycare and not your home or private belongings.

Most daycares have many tax advantages and though on paper you appear to not make a lot of money, you have a steady income each week. My insurance rate to cover my daycare was under $200 a year. When we moved to SC, we moved our coverage over. However, when it came time to do my taxes, I couldn't find the amount in my plan for my daycare. I called my insurance company only to find out they didn't cover in-home daycares in SC because of many lawsuits, so they dropped that from their plans in SC. I had no idea! I was told that if I continued to run my daycare out of my home, they would no longer cover my home or its contents. I was also told by the insurance company that most will not cover your home, etc. if you own a trampoline and certain breeds of dogs.

I began making calls and found another nationally recognized insurance company and moved all our plans over to them. We had lots of toys such as a boat, camper, jewelry, and life insurance policies, so they weren't very happy when we left them. Another option is, you can go online under daycareinsurance.com and find many daycare insurances companies who will cover you providing their questionnaire is filled out to their satisfaction.

Advertising for Daycare Openings

When I began in Daycare, I had to post ads in the newspaper or post on bulletin boards with my phone number in rows they could tear off. When Facebook started and the groups, along with craigslist, all that changed. It was expensive when I had to place an ad and to be honest, I rarely took anyone that answered an ad. I preferred referrals, and once I was established those were all I took, and I had a waiting list.

STORYTIME!

FAMILY #1 I had a woman answer my newspaper ad. She entered my home and struggled to take off her shoes as she was extremely obese. She had a son who was 4 years old. She was very cross with him about getting his shoes off and he was equally cross with her. During our interview, the child threw some toys at me and said I was stupid. The mother actually swore at the child. I knew I would not be taking this family and ended the interview at this time.

I stood up and told the child it was time to go put on his shoes as our time was ending. The mother looked surprised and huffed to the door. She fell on the floor trying to put her shoes on and could barely stand up and was swearing the entire time. She asked me how I could simply not take them. I informed her that this is my home and I need it to be a safe and harmonious atmosphere for my family and my daycare kids and considering how she and her son interact and how he spoke to me, it was not a good fit, and told her she needed to leave.

> **FAMILY #2** I had another family answer my newspaper ad. They drove up in a station wagon, and out came five children and the mother. They were ages 4-12 years old. They came in like a hurricane into my home! Two children immediately ran up the stairs to my upper level and another started opening my cabinets and closet doors. The mother said nothing! I called the kids upstairs to come down here immediately. They were rude and said something to the effect of "we were just checking out the place!" I told the one rummaging through my cabinets that that was not allowed. The mother had no control over the kids, but more importantly, she didn't see a need to stop any of their behavior. I asked them to follow me from the kitchen to the front door, I opened it and said they needed to leave. She swore at me and left.

This is YOUR HOME. You need to be okay with who comes to your home every day. Be very aware of their behavior, their language, their interactions with their child, and with you when you interview.

You will also have families who do not show up for their interviews. This is very frustrating. You have prepared your home, let family members know you need to have privacy for this. You may have a folder prepared with forms, etc. You wait, they don't call, and they don't show. You should save their information as you may get a call from them down the line and you will want to know if you can trust that they will show.

I made a point of telling families that if they can't make their appointment with me, please call and let me know as I will have prepared for their arrival. Most will, but some do not. It is what it is.

I also let them know the interview will last approximately 45 minutes. If you don't set a time, some will try and talk and talk and soon you are 90 minutes into it. That's not necessary. 45 minutes is plenty of time for all to meet, see your home, have a chat, and let them leave to make their decision. Now if they decide on the spot, they are signing with you, it may take a little longer as you go over what to bring and forms to fill out. But you will also be either giving them a hard copy of the

Program & Policy and Contract, or you will be emailing it to them along with the forms.

Reminder: This time preparing and conducting the interview is all time you record for your taxes. *More details on the interview process in Chapter 7: Interviewing.*

Chapter 2: Contracts

You are a business. You need a contract.

A contract is an agreement you make with another party and ensures clarity and protection to both parties. It states many things such as hours of service, weekly fees, deposit fees, late fees, starting dates, drop off and pick-up times, and an agreement to adhere to all the programs and policies you have supplied. You sign it, they sign, it's dated, and you now have a contract.

When I first started my daycare, I didn't even realize I needed a contract. I thought, "people are generally good, and they have concerns for their children and will be fair." I had one family who wouldn't show up several times within a week, and when I called to find out if they were coming to daycare (I was open at that time at 6 AM, which meant I was up at 5 AM to get ready) I was told, what difference did it make, they had paid me for the week. They were the only family I had at that hour of the morning so, yes, it did make a difference to me since I had to be up. I also had a family who decided on a Friday, that grandma was going to be taking care of the child as of Monday since she had lost her job, so since I didn't have a deposit, or contract, I had no income from that family the next week and had to place an ad, interview, and start to find a new family to make up the lost income as soon as possible.

I also had trouble with families picking up on time. They would decide to run errands before picking up, making them late. I even had a family who wrote me a bad check. It wasn't until we built our new home and moved next door to a woman who had been a daycare provider for 13 years, that I was mentored through the process of being a professional daycare provider. I learned that if I were professional, I would be treated (most of the time) professionally. I learned that a contract is very important as it not only gives me security, but it gives the daycare family accountability and security as well.

There were many times I called my friend next door and asked how to handle a difficult parent or child, how to deal with vacations (not only my own but also theirs), how to handle a part-time family when they want to change days to work around my paid time off for holidays, and the list goes on and on. I don't know what

I would have done without that support from a friend. I have also found through the years that just when I thought I had all the quirks worked out, a new situation would arise. But because I had done this for so long, I took a moment to really look at the situations before I answered and saved myself a lot of frustration. **This is why this book is important. We don't all live next door to a daycare or have someone with a veteran's knowledge of how to handle things.**

My contracts have changed over the years, I have added to them, edited some, added logos, and changed layouts. I had an inground pool and taught the kids to swim, so there was a signed contract needed for that to be able to allow kids in the pool. I would never run a business without a contract, ever.

I also had a form permitting the children to ride in my daycare van, a permission form to use photographs of their children in advertising, a permission form to go on outings to the park/zoo/waterpark/drive-thru/restaurants/museums, etc. Again, never wrong to be careful.

The children loved to go on trips to the zoo. In fact, in MN I would routinely take the children to the Minnesota Zoo and the Waterpark near my home. The permission forms included that the parents would be responsible for admission fees and most would simply purchase a season pass to the zoo and waterpark. Don't be concerned with asking for parents to cover these fees. Like field trips at school, most parents are thrilled to have their kid(s) exposed to museums, zoos, waterparks, and other activities and are more than willing to cover this. These activities should not come at your own expense. After all, you are covering the gas to get there, juice, snacks, etc. while out. Be sure to document these expenses for tax purposes as well.

Contract Violations

What if someone violates the contract?

If you can't resolve it so both parties are satisfied, your only recourse is to take them to small claims court. You will represent yourself, so keeping records is very important. Only you can determine if it is worth your time and worth the stress. In most cases, it's not.

So why have a contract? Because it keeps people honest, gives people accountability, and lets them know you are a serious businessperson and there is a possibility to have to answer in a court of law if it is violated. It also records the terms of your conversations, interviews, and agreements in writing, in case anyone forgets and needs to revisit the policies.

For example, deposits are a safeguard should someone give notice of leaving, but it's also a safeguard should *you* need to terminate without notice. The deposit is not returned but is paid upfront in order to cover the last 2 weeks of their daycare. If they terminate without notice it also serves as the 2 weeks needed to find someone to take their place.

Another example of a contracts' worth: Johnny is to be picked up every day at 4 p.m., but lately mom or dad is picking up at 4:30 p.m. and Johnny is your last child to be picked up from your daycare and your daughter has dance lessons at 4:30 p.m., so you are counting on families to be on time. You can then either talk to her and show her the agreed time and ask her to please abide by it, or you can make a copy of it, highlight the agreed time, and add a note that kindly explains the need to keep to the agreed pick-up time. Obviously, some will continue to violate the terms of the contract at which time you may need to terminate them from your daycare (*this is addressed in detail later with more options in Chapter 8: Terminating*).

I would suggest you go through these 4 steps first:

1. **Verbal reminder of terms** (document this in their file)
2. **Written reminder**
3. **Put them on probation** (1-2 weeks) and if there is still a problem, let them know the conflict you have on dance lesson day and if they can't pick up on time, they have to find another daycare and will owe you a late fee for that day as well.
    a. If they violate any terms during probation that is grounds for immediate termination. It functions as a warning.
4. **You terminate.** They do not receive their deposit back, as they have violated the contract.

For example, let's say I put the Smith family on probation for the next 2 weeks. I'll tell them, "If you pick up late again during the 2 weeks, I may have to terminate you. I don't want to, but I may need to." Then if they pick up late again, you can immediately terminate. Like any job, you're on a probationary period for 90 days and can be terminated immediately for any reason.

Side note on probationary periods: you can have a child on probation for the first 2-3 weeks of starting with your daycare. That way if a child that didn't seem irate at first later shows serious behavior issues you can terminate immediately.

If a family says, "well I'll just use my deposit during these 2 weeks and see if this works out." Then your response is "I'm sorry that's not how this works. I'm still paid every week including during your probationary period every Monday like before. Unless you are planning on giving me the 2-week notice now, then you may use your deposit. However, you still need to adhere to the Program and Policies that you have agreed upon. If you do not, the termination will happen immediately, and the rest of your deposit not used is forfeited. However, if something reasonable happens just give me a call and a heads up on what's going on. I can certainly work with you on situations that may come up out of your control." That way you still sound nice and reasonable—after all, we all have access to our phones nowadays and can give notice.

Without the immediate termination during the probationary period, they can still show up whenever the heck they want, use their deposit up, and leave at the end of the 2 weeks. The immediate termination allows you to keep the deposit during the probationary period and not get screwed.

If the Smith family calls with a genuine emergency or situation saying, "Hey I can't get out of this meeting" or "I'm stuck in traffic", those are reasonable life situations even during a probationary period. It all boils down to having mutual respect for one another. This creates a good working and personal relationship with families that fosters long-term relationships and referrals.

Others don't care whether they pay for late fees because they can afford it. This is also not favorable if you need to get to your kid's soccer practice or any other appointment you may have. You also have a right to start your evening with your family at a certain time. You don't want to allow repeat violations simply because they can afford it. It got to a point with one family where I had to say "Look, if you can't pick up your kid on time, I'll have to take them with me to my child's practice and you can pick up BillyBob from there." I made an exception for this family because they had been with me for a long time and we had become friends. But that's your right as a business owner to make exceptions for some people or some situations and decide what's worth it and what's not.

Contract Modification

Parents occasionally find loopholes in the contract and you'll need to modify contracts.

At the end of my Program and Policies, I have a modification clause that states that my Program and Policies can be modified at any time. Families will be notified of the update and the updated version will take precedence over any previous Program and Policies. The Program and Policies document works together with the contract.

Again, if you are professional, you will most times be treated as such. Situations like the one explained above, are a good example of how to enforce your contract agreement. Once a family understands that you will address situations when they arise and not wait to see if things change, they become accountable, and your relationship stays professional and clear. Keep in mind, no daycare center would allow issues like this. Once you let it slide, you have lost your credibility.

Another example: If a family is giving their 2-week notice, you have the 2-week deposit. However, if you haven't used your accumulated PTO a.k.a. VBR (Vacation Balance Reconciliation) for the time they have been in daycare, you are owed that as it accrues monthly. You take the amount of the PTO accrued and add that to your amount owed to you.

So, let's say you have a 2-week deposit and 3 days of PTO earned (but not used), you give them (*in writing*) the amount they owe for that to be paid upfront before leaving. They are using their 2-week deposit for their last 2 weeks of daycare payment, so they won't be paying you for those last 2 weeks, however, they still owe you for time not used in PTO. That needs to be paid upfront to secure daycare for the next 2 weeks. *An example letter given to a previous family in my care is included with the forms at the end of this book.*

Not all daycares do this. I did this in the latter part of my years in the business. I implemented this since I would frequently have a family or a couple of families leave my daycare right before I was going to take my vacation (so they wouldn't have to pay me while I was on vacation), thus I was out the PTO earned from this family. Look at it this way, if you were working for a corporation and gave your 2-weeks' notice at work, you would be paid for your last 2 weeks plus any unused PTO earned. It's the same thing.

Chapter 3: Program and Policies

You need to create a Program & Policy Booklet to use or to simply use as a guide. This outlines what your daycare day is like for a typical day. An example of this will be with forms and templates at the end of this book.

- An outline of the day (morning snack time, lunch, afternoon snack).
- Nap times are for certain age groups.
- What they should bring daily in their bags, or what they should keep at daycare should it be needed.
- A sick policy.

Sick Policy

A sick policy is one of the most important parts of the program and policy you have in your booklet!! I found that it's best to use what most schools use since it's reasonable.

1. Contagious illnesses must be kept at home until no medication is needed for 24 hours.
2. If your child has a fever of over 101°F, they will be separated from the group and you will be called to pick up.
3. If your child has more than one diarrhea instance, you will be called to pick up.
4. Any rashes/hives or unexplained blotches and you will be called to pick up.
5. At times children will run a slight fever with teething or have a small amount of diarrhea. If it is felt this is from teething, there will be no need for a call.
6. If your child has a chronic cough, bark-like cough (croup), along with green mucus from the nose, you will be called to pick up.
7. Children can have allergies, and noses will run clear if there is no infection and is not infectious.
8. If your child is not feeling well enough to participate in normal activities during the day, this is reason to keep them home until they are well.
9. No child will have their symptoms masked with medication, as this will wear off over a few hours and they will have already exposed the other children to their illness.

10. If a child comes with prescription meds or over the counter meds, it must be in the actual prescribed bottle. You should also have a form you supply signed by both you and the parent designating the dosage. Be sure to have this form already drafted as a template as you may not be prepared when this occurs. A parent could arrive and tell you over the weekend the child came down with a cough, etc. and we are giving them this medication.

You may come up with more of your own, but it is important that this is in your policy.

> **STORYTIME!**
> The time this proved to be very important to me was when I had a family with a child under 2 years old. She was extremely fussy for two days, nothing was helping, and I had all the other kids to take care of. It wasn't fair to them because this one was consuming all my attention and I was having to put movies in for the kids instead of doing our normal routine. After day two, I told mom she needed to have her child seen by a doctor before returning. She was very annoyed with me. The following day she called me, and I could hear her child crying terribly in the background. Mom informed me that her child had two broken eardrums! She told me she had some drops for her and pain meds, and that she would be at my place in about 20 minutes. What?! No way! I informed her that she couldn't bring her child here today. When she said to me that her child didn't have anything contagious as my sick policy states, I reminded her that it also states, "If your child ... (above #8 and #9)" She was very angry. I reminded her that her child needed her mom and her undivided attention right now, and when her child felt better and meds were helping, she could return. She gave her two weeks' notice two days later. I was fine with that. You need to be okay when a situation arises like that. It's for your sanity as well as the well-being of your daycare. Other parents will appreciate you protecting their children from the unnecessary spread of illnesses.

Because I had the sick policy in my Program and Policy, I was protected in stating the child could not come to daycare at this time.

EVERY time... I feel I have my program and policy booklet up to par on all issues... SOMETHING ELSE pops up! I dealt with it and added it if I felt it was needed on how to deal with it. Towards the end, I didn't have to add anything. Hopefully, you will find you do not need to face all the challenges I have over the years and you can be prepared for most situations because this book was designed to do just that! At the end of this book, I will have template forms that I have used to help you formulate yours.

Having a Program & Policy is vital to any business. It is used as a reference when questions arise, as proof of policy, and to compare your business to someone else's. You will be prepared, look professional, and impress your interviewing families. After all, if you were taking your children to someone, wouldn't you want to feel they are qualified and have a Program?

I was constantly asked during an interview if I have a Sick Policy in my daycare. Usually, it is because they have experienced a previous daycare that allowed children who are very ill to remain in care, which means, most of the children will also become ill. That means ill and unhappy children, time lost from work, co-pays at the doctor, prescriptions to be purchased, etc. Occasionally, but not often, it is asked because they are the parent who wants their children to be cared for even if they become ill or are ill. They feel they have paid for daycare and that should be part of the program. That may be true of some daycares, but it has never been my practice.

I informed my prospective families that I am not a clinic, I am a daycare. If the child isn't up to participating in normal activities, they should be home, along with other obvious symptoms of illness such as fever. I also let them know I am aware that some parents will medicate their children and bring them anyway. That usually doesn't last long, and if the child is older, they usually will let me know, and I will be calling for the parents to come and pick up.

Now, I am not talking about someone who gives meds because of a slight cough or teething. I am referring to medicating for a fever, "masking" the symptoms so they can get some time put in at work. I have caught several families over the years trying to pull one over on me, and they were always found out and I let them know that I would not tolerate this. I gently explain, if someone else's child were sick with fever and I allowed them to remain at daycare then their child would most likely get sick. Would they really want that? Most don't. Very few will say "they need to be exposed, it will help them later"--what they are really saying is: they want or need to go to work and this is inconvenient.

When a child becomes ill, whether the child's symptoms were masked with medication or they simply became ill while in daycare, you will want to remove them from the area the other children are at, but also still be able to keep them within your sight. Maybe lay them on a family room sofa or a sleeping mat in the next room until a parent/guardian can come to pick them up. The lesser the exposure to the other kids, the better.

Permission Forms

These days, permission forms are necessary for everything. If you have a child in school, you know this to be true. Similar to a Program & Policy Booklet, Permission Forms serve as written proof of permission and protect you. Permission forms are necessary to travel outside of the daycare to the local park, library, to take photos of the children at play to share with the group and with the families, or a webpage you may have, or an advertisement of your daycare. A permission form to use a monitor on a sleeping child while you are tending to the other children is important.

For example, if you decide to travel on a field trip without written permission and the parent hasn't been made aware, you could be in serious trouble with the county and that parent. If you should have an accident while traveling, you most likely will have a lawsuit against you. Permission forms are essential. Better safe than sorry. Again, you can never be too careful and that goes for protecting yourself too.

Immunizations:

I insisted that all children must be up to date with their immunizations to be allowed into my daycare. I received calls at times from parents asking if I required this. The parents who do not agree with immunizations would understand that I will not accept their child. I found that almost all families were happy that this was required.

Chapter 4: Running a Daycare during COVID-19

You need to stay safe and keep your families safe, but they also need to keep you safe. Obviously, good cleansing and disinfecting is part of daycare even without a pandemic. Keeping the toys, door handles, bathrooms, and hands clean is important. Having a conversation or sending a note or email to parents indicating what your plans are to help keep everyone as safe as possible with COVID-19 would be appropriate. I would also add that you hope they are practicing safety precautions as well to keep you safe too. With this new issue of COVID-19 all of us are facing globally, there are extra precautions you should be taking. Each state will have listed on their DHS site the guidelines to adhere to. The following are some possible ideas you can implement into your daily routine and ask for your families support in this endeavor:

1. Taking your daycare kids temperature upon arrival (forehead thermometer for sanitary reasons).
2. Taking their temperature at least one more time halfway through their day.
3. If parents do not want to have their temperature taken, they can stand on the step or sidewalk and let their child enter with your assistance.
4. Have children go immediately to the bathroom and wash their hands with antibacterial soap for at least 20 seconds.
5. Should a child develop a fever, they need to be placed separate from the other children and you. Then immediately call their parents to pick up. As with all fevers, they need to be fever free 24 hours without meds.
6. Watch for the very young ones to have rashes anywhere on their little bodies.
7. Keep field trips to a minimum and preferably an outdoor venue.
8. Be sure to wash all children's hands immediately upon leaving the venue and when returning to the vehicle or house. Hand sanitizer works well when you're traveling to a park and don't have a sink available yet.
9. If you want to be very diligent, when going to a park, bring disinfectant wipes and wipe down what you can before the children play.

10. Be sure door handles, toilet handles, stair railings, counter tops are cleaned with disinfectant/alcohol wipes at the beginning/end of each day.
11. If the children bring their own lunches, wipe down their lunchbox if one is used.
12. When possible, weather permitting, play and learn outside. If inside, choose to spend most of the time in a large room.
13. Avoid games that promote the children from holding hands or making close contact.

Chapter 5: Rates

I would suggest that you have a Rate Sheet. I have supplied an example along with other forms for your reference at the back of this book. Rates will change over the years, and honestly, they should increase yearly. Take into account your state, your area, where your families are coming from, and possibly make some calls to other daycares and ask about their rates. Some private home daycares don't like to tell other daycares their rates, so I can honestly say that I have called as if I was a prospective family looking for a daycare to get that information. You can always have a friend with children make a call for you.

Some counties will supply you with a rate sheet based on towns, cities, and areas. Remember, however, these are not always completely accurate. It's best to check the rates of centers, home daycares, and church daycares and go from there to decide your own. During the last 8 years, I raised my rates by $5.00/week annually. It's not so much that anyone objects but enough in the weekly rate and monthly rate that you feel the increase.

Also, check the daycare centers for reference. They will always be much higher priced than you and that is good information to have at interview time if the parents bring up an issue with your rates. You can come back with "well, I know that centers are charging x rate and I'm still below that rate." I also let families know, if my rates are a little higher, it's because my daycare is also a learning daycare, complete with the preschool program, field trips, t-shirts, etc. I have a high standard for my daycare and my families appreciate that their kids don't just run and play all day or sit and watch T.V. There are many daycares where that is the case. Kids also learn that there are some things in a home that are off-limits, and I also taught table manners as well. Therefore, their child is learning at-home etiquette and table manners as well. Sell your daycare! You have a great program, own that!

Rates are priced at full-time, part-time, and drop-in rates. You may also have summer rates for a family that has another child that needs to come because school is out or during the school year when school is closed. At one time I gave a discount to families with more than one child in my care. It was a 10% discount. I stopped that because of two reasons: 1) I could have a child from another family at full rate, and 2) if the family with more than one leaves, it leaves me with several spots to fill. So, I stopped. Financially, it made no sense.

The same goes for a family who wants only a few hours a day versus a family who wants a full day. For example, you have a family that wants BillyBob to come to daycare from 9 a.m. to 1 p.m. and wants to pay a discounted rate because they are not in daycare all day. What are the chances of you having another child to fill that same spot from 1 p.m. - 5 p.m. for the remainder of the day to make up the difference in wage lost? Very, very small.

So, I came up with what I feel is very reasonable and I have had little objection to it when I explain that I do not have discounted rates for a portion of the day. I have a 3-day minimum required for my daycare, whether they are in my care for 2 days or 3. The family, who has their child in my care 5 days a week pays a lower daily rate because they are consistent. The family who is in my care 4 days a week pays a slightly higher daily rate, and the same goes for the daily family who is in my care for 3 days. Obviously, the family who needs care for only 2 days pays a higher rate for those 2 days because of the 3-day minimum I require. But I have to make it financially worth my while because I could have that spot filled with a full-time, 5 day-a-week family. Where otherwise I would have given a spot 2-3 days a week and have a couple of days where it may be difficult to fill. Therein lies the reasoning for the higher rate and the 3-day minimum.

You may say, "*well, it would be nice to have a lighter group of children some days.*" While that may be true, only you can decide what your rates are, but you will find others in your area help make that decision for you. There will always be that daycare that has the "lowest rates in town" and some will be very high. I never apologize for my rates because I know I run a good daycare and after I interview with them, they know I do too.

Also compare with what services they offer and what you are willing to offer. Do they have a preschool program? Do they provide snacks and/or lunch? Do they have holiday programs (Christmas party, Easter egg hunt)? If not, you can more easily justify higher rates during the interview.

Don't get hung up on the "per hour"

Refer to Babysitters vs. Daycare Providers in Chapter 6.

One thing I would suggest you *don't* do is this: do not get hung up on what you are making *per hour* for each child.

For example: Say you charge $100 per week for a child who is in your care 10 hours a day, 5 days a week--that comes to $2.00 per hour. It sounds pretty low, I agree, but you need to look at the weekly rate to feel okay with the rates. That is how rates are typically charged. Don't worry... examples below will make you feel much better about your income!

Don't fret...remember that the $100/week is per child. If you have 6 children in your care, that's $600 per week. $600 divided by 50 hours per week = $12/hour. So again, don't get caught up on the per hour for each child. To be clear, I am using $100/week as an example to keep the math simple, I charged more than $100/week.

The rates will vary since different aged children will have different rates, so not every child is $100 per week regardless of age. At the end of this book, I have a full Rate Template with a breakdown of what I charged for different age groups that you can use as a guide. So really, you'd be making much more than $12/hour considering the higher rates for other children.

Example: 6 children: 1 infant at $190/week, 3 toddlers at $181/week, 1 preschool at $171/week, and 1 school age at $150/week = $1,054 per week (divided by 50 hours is $21.08 per hour). That's pretty decent! And that's just for 6 children!

In Minnesota, you can have up to 12 children in your care! Double that and you have $42/hour (calculated at all children at full-time in this example). So, don't worry about $2/week per kid and look at the bigger picture for your income as well as the large tax deductions.

INFANTS (6 weeks – 12 months)
$190/week (5 Days)
$135/3 days
$45/drop in (1 day)

TODDLER (1 year – 3 years)
$181.00/week (5 days)
$120.00/3 days

PRESCHOOL (3 years – 5 years, not in kindergarten)
$171.00/week (5 days)
$114.00/3 days

SCHOOL AGE (5 years in kindergarten – 10 years)
   (during summer or when school is out for vacation)
$150.00/week (5 days)
$105.00/3 days

SCHOOL AGE (during the school year)
Before School only: $60/week
After School only: $75/week includes snack
Before & After School: $90/week, includes after school snack

**taken from the Rates Template at the back of the book (rates estimate for Minneapolis, MN in 2020)*

If you charged minimum wage at $7.25/hour per kid, you'd be charging $362.50 per week and parents just aren't going to pay that. That's $1,450 per month per child, as opposed to $400 per month for the parent(s) to pay. Much more reasonable. Again, $400/month just an example to keep math simple.

So, when you're having an issue with parents on your rates, then you can make it clear that they are only paying you ~$2/hour for their child (varies). That will put it in perspective as to what they are ***actually*** paying you per hour for their child in daycare. Obviously the per hour rate would be based upon the actual rate you are charging.

Infant/Baby's Rates

Babies are always in high demand for daycare. I could have filled a baby spot in my daycare weekly. Centers are busy and have waiting lists and are very expensive typically. Most parents do not want their baby in a busy center or a home daycare with lots of children. A smaller home daycare environment is ideal for an infant.

A baby's rate can vary but can be quite profitable as well. Many centers charge as much as $350 a week or more for infants, depending upon your area.

STORYTIME!
One year I took a set of twin girls into my care. Since they were born in January to a local P.E. teacher at our high school, I knew this would be a short-term arrangement and the twins would possibly return in the fall. I also was aware that she would have been quoted very high rates to care for her infants in centers, and most daycare homes would not probably take her children. I charged her a higher rate because I was doing double duty, literally. I normally would have charged at that time (1999) $150/week, but because there were two babies, I charged $200 per week, per child. The parents told me I was $50 less per week, per child than any other quote and she signed on. I was fortunate that those girls were so good, so easy to care for, and I almost felt guilty for the rate....almost. :) My license in MN allowed me to take two infants if I cut back my allowed 12 children to 10, and I was only allowed one toddler while the rest had to be

> preschool and older. So, when all things considered, it made sense for me to charge what I did to make up for two fewer children than normally allowed. It was Minnesota's way of safeguarding the child for ultimate care in a home daycare setting.

Your state will have a rule of how many children are allowed according to their age groups. My Minnesota license allowed: 1 infant, 2-3 toddlers, 4 preschools, and 4 school-age children for a total of 12 children at any given time. That's where full-time and part-time come in handy.

I have had as many as 14 children on my roster, but never more than 12 at a time in my care. Babies are wonderful little beings. They smell good, they sleep a lot, they coo, and cuddle... but they are also time-consuming. They come with many demands, whether formula or breastmilk fed, they require extra attention and more time. They dictate your day and your activities. They also bring added stress such as SIDS to be aware of.

Monitors are a necessity. Some states will not allow you to even get your mail while an infant is sleeping while others will allow you to wear a monitor. If your county allows a monitor for outside use, I recommend you have a permission form signed by both parents regardless. Remember, you can never be too careful!

I used a monitor even for my older children who may be napping while I am outside with older children or on a different floor of our home. Even with a monitor, it is wise to check periodically on an infant during naptime to be sure all is well--that blankets are not over the child's face for example.

The SIDS program discourages the use of blankets at all for babies in their crib. It is best if they sleep in a zip-up bunting. Most counties will not allow bumper pads, pillows of any kind, stuffed animals, or any kind of soft toy in the crib with the infant as a precaution to any possibility of suffocation to the child.

When I had the twin girls in my care, though the parents had them sleep in the same crib at home, that is NOT allowed, at least in MN it wasn't. I checked because I knew I would be introducing them to a new sleeping arrangement and that could change things quite a bit for them and me. I was concerned that they wouldn't sleep well. But the State was very clear, so I had to get a loaner crib so they would each have their own crib. They did sense each other in the room and their cooing and baby talk to each other helped them settle into slumber. They didn't even wake the other one if one cried.

In my tenth year of daycare, I decided not to take any more babies for many reasons. One major reason was the stress of SIDS, it can and will break your daycare should it happen to you. If it happens, the authorities are called and parents of course. They have all children removed from your care until an investigation takes place. There will be something in the paper or on the news regarding this. People will think that there was foul play. Even if it is determined to be a real SIDS case, which one cannot do anything about, it will make the newspaper, and most won't know whether or not you have been cleared of any foul play. You will lose your daycare families, marriages split up, sometimes you can lose your house with no income. Because I attended monthly meetings for daycare providers, I met some people who had experienced this. The second reason was that my own children were getting older, so I loved going on field trips with the kids and doing crafts which is so much easier without an infant in your care.

A few years later, I bent my own rule as I had a couple of my daycare families become pregnant and I didn't want to lose them, so I took the babies again. I did, however, use a swing most of the time for naps. And the swing was in the room with me so I could watch the baby always as they slept. If the baby slept in the crib, I found something I could do in the room where the baby was sleeping to personally monitor them.

Sudden Infant Death Syndrome (SIDS)

Most states will require you to take a SIDS class along with your CPR and First Aid Class. I would suggest that even if your state or county does not require it, to take it anyway. That way you are educated in case of a need and your daycare families will have confidence in you to know you have taken the extra step to be sure of their child's safety.

The classes are all worth their weight in gold. Hopefully, you will never need to use any of them, other than the normal bumps and scrapes that a little Neosporin, band-aid, and kiss and hug can't take care of. They are all interesting classes, and you will meet others in your field of work as well as parents, coaches, and students. The cost is relatively inexpensive. When I did this, it was approximately $45-$75 per class depending upon your area.

Chapter 6: Hours of Operation

You need to decide how many hours you plan to run your daycare per day. You want to be convenient to families and their work schedules and their travel time to and from work, but you must also be considerate of your own family's needs as well. When I first opened my daycare, the first family I interviewed needed daycare at 6 a.m. So instead of continuing to interview until I found a family with a later start time, I agreed to the 6 a.m. schedule. This meant I was up at 5 a.m. to get ready and prepare for their arrival. I was also open until 6 p.m. because of the daycare families' needs. After the first six months of running my daycare, I established different hours that worked better with my own family. I was open at 7 a.m. and closed at 5:30 p.m.

A couple of years later when I was established, I found that I could change my closing to 5:00 p.m. Monday through Thursday and 4 p.m. on Fridays. When you have a two-parent family, one usually can make that happen. One parent will drop off and the other will pick up usually. It worked out well with the families I had at the time, plus I had a waiting list I could draw from should a family decide to leave. *Remember* by Thursday at 5 p.m. you already have 40 hours of work in for the week and by Friday another 9 hours! I found if they really want your daycare, they will find a way to make it work.

The year we bought a camper, I presented to my families an idea of being closed on Fridays in the summer and that they would only pay the 4 days a week rate. They had no issue with this at all! If they had to, they took PTO from work or changed their schedules to coincide with my daycare hours. It was only for the summer anyway. It was great for my family because we would leave Thursday night after daycare and go camping through Sunday. Best decision ever! Another perk to owning your own business is the ability to do things like this.

You need to realize your needs are important as well. A stressed and overworked Daycare Provider isn't a good provider. Time with family and free time are mentally and physically important. As my children grew, things were added to our schedules such as dance lessons, gymnastics, soccer, and music lessons. So, having a set time when daycare is over is important. One of the reasons I went to

Fridays closing at 4 p.m. during the school year was so that I could make doctor, dentist, nail, and haircut appointments. And it meant I didn't interfere with my daycare families' schedules.

Late Pickups

So, what happens when they pick up late? If your daycare family picks up late and you have an appointment, that can be a problem. A couple of times I was turned away from appointments because I was late getting there. You must realize you are running a business. Yes, it's a home, but it is a business. You pay taxes, you have business hours, you have expenses. So, treat it as such.

I would tell my families I can usually work through a bump in the road with compromise, but not with my hours. My family deserves my undivided attention at the end of the day, and so did my husband. But more importantly, you deserve to have some time to yourself, to close the doors to business, and to have dinner with your family. If you are open at 7 a.m. - 5 p.m., that is a 10-hour day. You may have a family that needs to be reminded that though they may be dropping their child off after 8 a.m. or later, you have been working since 7 a.m.

> **STORYTIME!**
> I once had a family in my care, where the mom had changed her hours at work. She was going to be working until 6 p.m. and wanted me to extend my daycare hours to accommodate her hours. I tried to explain to her that I work 10 hours a day and would not be adding to that. She said, and I quote, "it's only daycare". I held my tongue and suggested that she find other care that would meet her needs for her new hours. You will be amazed at times what is said to you. But keep your cool, keep professional and keep in mind, you have a very important job. You are caring for someone's child, their most prized possession. And daycare is very important, even if some do not view it as such.

Babysitter vs. Daycare Provider

This has come up so many times in my years of daycare this section gets its own heading under hours! LOL! It's already come up twice in this book!

It bears repeating: Many times, over the years, I have had to correct individuals who refer to me as a "babysitter". I tell them, I am a daycare provider, not a sitter. And when asked to explain the difference, I say "a sitter is someone you call when you are going to a movie, who sits with your child for a couple of hours, makes a respectable, hourly wage, and usually is a young teenager or elderly person".

I am a full-time daycare provider, with years of experience, not only as a mother but as a provider, with education in the field. This is my livelihood. I am First Aid, CPR, SIDS, certified. I not only play with the children, but I direct them, guide them, and teach them. I am a consistent role model in their lives. I am a counselor, referee, confidant, and I am like a mother to them. And then I add with a wink and a smile, "but if you would like to call me a babysitter and pay me at their hourly rate, I wouldn't object". They never took me up on that.

Full-Time and Part-Time

I always accepted both full- and part-time families for a few reasons. First, it is sometimes difficult to find only full-time children. Second, some days will be lighter, and this can be a nice change during the week. Third, you can have a variety of hours, personalities, and make a little extra money where a full-time child's spot has not been filled. It also offers flexibility to families who quite often these days work from home several days a week. Many centers will not accept part-time families, which in turn makes home daycare popular.

Babies

Babies/Infants age 1 day to 12 months.

I would however caution you on taking babies any less than 3 days a week. Quite often, the baby schedule at home will be different than that at daycare. A happy baby in daycare is a baby with consistent routines. During interviews with expectant parents or parents with babies, I suggest that we both try to be on the same schedule so the baby will be happy. I typically have babies schedule as follows:
- Nap time: 9 to 10/10:30 a.m.
- Then up for play
- Then lunchtime
- Naptime again no later than 1 p.m. to ~3 p.m.

I explain that if mom and dad try to keep the same schedule at home, their baby will be happier, and they won't have trouble during weekends. Obviously, weekends can be busy with mixed up schedules, visitors, and trips out. So, I usually expect babies to be a little off on their first day back to daycare for the week.

Chapter 7: Interviewing

Look the part if you were going to an office you would dress appropriately, it is the same when running your daycare! Your families want to know you are ready for their child's arrival and have a great day planned for them. Be dressed in comfortable casual clothes, not pajama pants, wear a smile at their arrival, and be upbeat. After all, they are entrusting you with their child, and want to feel good when they leave for work, that everyone is excited about the day.

Interviewing the parent _and_ the child. This is a very important part of setting up your daycare. Remember, *you are interviewing the prospective family* as much as they are interviewing *you!* The child needs to be *with* the parents at the interview. If a family asks to interview without their child present, it would be wise to simply suggest rescheduling at a time when all can be present. Sometimes it is a red flag if the parents don't want the child present at the interview.

There could be a behavior problem; there may be a physical/mental issue that the parents do not wish to inform you of. This is a sensitive area; compassion yet realistic attitudes need to be upfront. I found that if I was completely honest with a prospective parent of, for example, a child with special needs that would require lifting, I explained that I was not able to lift heavy objects or children because I have a back injury and was under chiropractic care. You may always choose to interview, see how everyone feels, trust your instincts and let everyone always know that though there may be an opening, you will need to interview everyone interested and make your assessment of what will fit into your program and your personal daycare needs. If you promise to call them either way, be sure you do that. **Remember, this is your home as well as your daycare business. They must be in harmony.**

Sometimes I interview even if I did not have an opening at the time. It's always wise to have options, and even to have a back-up list for openings that arrive, due to departures, starting school, and terminations. I have interviewed parents who are in the early stages of pregnancy and want to have their daycare set up ahead of time. I have found these parents to be very conscientious and good families for daycare.

Special Needs

Understand, once in a while, you may run into a family who has had a difficult time finding daycare for their child or children because of special needs. Check with your DSS to see if you are required to take someone with special needs if you have an opening. Some states could require you to, and also require you to alter your home to fit their needs. Personally, I found DSS to be very understanding, and when I would get a call from either them or a state service asking if I had experience with a child with special needs, depending on what that need was, I let them know if I was or not. If not, they didn't recommend my daycare to that family.

I also once interviewed a family of a child with MRSA, a highly contagious skin disease. She didn't tell me initially. We were in my playroom having our interview. I noticed a few band-aids on the child and asked him about it. He pulled up his shirt and they were everywhere. Luckily, we were at the end of the interview and told her as she was leaving that I am sure it's hard to find a daycare, but I can't take her child as it would have a risk to my other children and myself. She tried to complain to DSS about me. Since DSS had a copy of my Program and Policy Booklet they were aware of my sick policy. Also, the parent hadn't planned on letting me know her child's condition. There was no issue, and I wasn't forced to take her child.

Taking Friends/Relatives into your Daycare

The story you read earlier in Sick Policy was about a personal friend of mine. She had heard many stories of my daycare at social gatherings and the frustrations I had. When she had her child, she said she wanted her to come to my daycare. I told her I don't take friend's kids, as it is a problem to separate friendship and business and not have it affect the relationship.

She went on to tell me she would never do some of the things she has heard about from me and insisted I take on her child. Regrettably, I did, and our friendship was over after the issue.

Now, there is a huge difference in _becoming_ friends with daycare families. Becoming being the operative word here. The business side of things has already been established. You simply need to not change how you do business with them because you have become friends outside of daycare.

> **STORYTIME!**
>
> An example of 'becoming' friends is the following. A woman I will call Victoria came to me days before school was to begin in the fall. She had her grandson with her. She had heard about me from the school and came to the interview. She had a unique situation. The mother of her grandson had left the child (10 mos.) with Victoria and her husband and wasn't coming back. She needed immediate daycare. Victoria and her husband eventually adopted the child. Victoria was a great daycare parent and a great mom. We soon became friends and had much in common. We socialized a lot--pool parties, vacations at Myrtle Beach, New Year's parties. We were friends. It did not change how I did daycare, my rules didn't change, and she never took advantage of me as the business part of our relationship came first and was established. We are still friends sixteen years later.

There were several families over the years where this was the same case. Our kids were friends as well. They spent overnights and we socially all hung out together. No one ever stepped over the line for special treatment.

Chapter 8: Termination

Terminating a family from your daycare. My program had a 3-week trial period. This period is used to determine if the fit of your daycare and the child/parents are a good fit. There are times when certain behaviors do not show themselves in an interview. There may be situations that were not disclosed. For example, a child with a behavioral problem that is treated with medication.

> **STORYTIME!**
>
> I once had an extremely destructive child, and though I tried daily to work with the family, I felt I wasn't being heard. It became obvious that this child's father (who was the only parent) was not directly involved with the child and left that responsibility to his friend and his friend's wife. By the end of week three, the child had busted my oldest daughter's lip and broke the eyeglasses of one of the daycare kids and I terminated our agreement immediately. Only then did I hear from the father of the child. Having my Program & Policy in place was my safety net and DSS stood behind me 100 percent.

I can honestly say that in the 21 years of daycare, I terminated less than 8 families. Usually, it is not because of the child, but because of the parent. They either are continually late picking up, not paying on time, writing bad checks, not following policies, etc.

A Note on Recordkeeping

Always document any and all occurrences with the child AND with the parents. Keep a file on *every* child. The file is where you will store a copy of your contract, permissions forms, immunizations, photos, etc. it is imperative to keep accurate and updated records on children in your care. *I will get into more detail on this in Chapter 9: Recordkeeping.*

Dealing with difficult parents

There will be times when certain families will present you with situations that are out of the normal routine. This particular parent will most likely ask you to do things or make changes during a busy time like during drop off or pick-up times when it is difficult to think without interruption.

When this happens, I would suggest you handle it like this: "you know, I would love to give you an answer to this right now, but because things are a bit hectic right now, (or maybe more children are about to arrive) let me give you a call or text later today or tonight and see if that is something I can do if possible." Don't let them pressure you for an answer right at the moment. Even if it's time-sensitive, just let them know you will get back to them as soon as daycare settles today, and you have a chance to see if their request works for you. That way, you are not answering something you will kick yourself for later.

I can't tell you how many times this happened to me over the early years. I was talked out of paid holidays, vacations, and added children to my care for days expected to be lighter because of a holiday in the week, or other reasons. And only after I would say "oh, that's okay", would I realize later that I just agreed to something that was taking money or convenience from myself, and knowing full well that the family requesting this already knew how this would affect me and benefit them because they had time to think about what they wanted or needed. Take the time to say: **"I will get back to you on that"**.

If this seems confusing let me give you a quick example of an actual situation.

> **STORYTIME!**
> I had a family who has contracted for 4 days a week: Monday - Thursday. You think, great schedule; I have Fridays off from this one family which of course makes a lighter load at the end of the week. My contract says I'm paid for ALL holidays listed in the Program & Policy booklet and if they fall on a weekend, I will take a day close to that date as the holiday such as a Monday or Friday with notice.
> Example: July 4th falls on a Monday. What this means is: Monday is a paid holiday and daycare is closed. But your Monday through Thursday family who pays for 4 days a

> week wants to change that for this week only. They want Tuesday through Friday; thus, you lose out on fewer kids on your typical Friday and if you agree, you aren't paid from them on Monday for your paid holiday off.
>
> If you held to your agreement, they would still pay you the normal weekly rate, but would only come Tuesday through Thursday that week and you would still have your paid-time-off day as listed in your Program & Policies under Holidays/Vacations/Sick Time.
>
> I had a family who had pulled this on me several times, and each time I was so mad at myself. After she had left my daycare because her son was now school age and she worked her hours so she would be home when he came home on the bus, she contacted me after the birth of her second son. I was ready for her this time. Again, she wanted Monday through Thursday. I said that would be fine, here is the rate...and just to make you aware, that schedule does not change regardless of holidays, so if a holiday falls within those days, daycare is closed, and I am still paid your regular weekly rate. I never heard back from her. I had their first son in my care for 4½ years mind you. Then she gave a neighbor a bad review for my daycare who ended up coming to my daycare regardless. They told me about it and said they had a feeling she was angry (about something not going her way) at the interview.

Now, if you wanted to accommodate them, you could simply offer this without losing money, but you would still have a heavier Friday than originally scheduled since her child or children would be there.

You also need to consider, if you have regular "drop-ins" (a child who comes periodically on a given day, or if you get calls for drop-ins regularly) you will most likely not have the space for the "drop-in", thus you miss out on added income. So, what you would say would be something like: *"Okay, you can bring BillyBob on Friday, but since I have Monday as a paid holiday and you contracted for Mon-Thurs., for me to have my paid holiday, you can simply add the daily rate of [$....] to your check for that week."* And be sure they always pay at the beginning of a week.

Nine times out of ten, they will say; *"oh, well, we will work something else out, because we can't afford to (or we don't want to pay more)"* or *"That's fine, we will work something else out".*

But keep in mind, if you do relinquish your paid holidays, you have opened the door to other situations that will fall short of your contract, and why have one giving you benefits if you do not enforce them. So, be wary of people who want to discuss a change during a busy time or want an answer right away because of the need at the moment, it is usually not in your best interest.

Chapter 9: Recordkeeping

Keeping records on children

As stated previously in Chapter 4, this is a *very important* part of the business. Start a file on each child AT the interview. I kept one file for the interview candidates. I make notes when receiving calls and jot down information, such as the age of the child, when they need care, are they in a center or home now? What hours are they looking for? Anything that will help me at the interview if it leads to that.

Even if the interview doesn't take place, or if it does and they do not contract with you, they may in the future, and it's good to have information at hand that they have shared with you previously.

When they sign with your daycare, their name is put on a new file. I also write their date of birth and start date on the tab, this is convenient for when you are doing tax work, or forms for the county each year. You may even want to write full time or part-time.

Inside the folder is the signed contract/admission form, permission forms, immunization forms, photo of the child if given, or you may take one and put it in their file. I keep all cards and notes as well from the family or the child in that file as well. For example, if a child or parent has a situation or injury, I make detailed notes of the situation and keep that in the file as well.

I also have a file on my computer on each child as I will be creating their tax forms each year and it works together. If you send a note home for a parent in the child's bag, make a copy of that as well if you don't have a copy machine. Make a note in the file of what you sent home with the child.

Also, keep special notes from families and children because it can then be used as back up if they claim that they were not happy with your daycare. And quite possibly if they decide they don't like a policy, etc., you have some proof that they were happy with your daycare and that you did things they claim didn't happen.

Example of something to take note of in a child's file: The child shows up with an obvious bruise. I would get down to the child's level and say something like "oh boy! What happened here?" If the child is of talking age, they will be eager to tell you. If they shy from telling you, or the parent answers for the child, this *can* be a red flag. Make note of the bruise and the conversation and how it went.

If it is a child who is too young to talk, I ask the parent directly. I make note of their explanation in the file. Now, be careful not to sound accusing, you are simply making small talk with someone you know and care for. It should sound natural. You may come across a mark or bruise on a child at diaper changing time. Make note of that in that file. When the parent picks up, I would mention what you found and what time of day it was when you noticed it.

Example: *"this morning shortly after you left, BillyBob needed a diaper change-- or "Billy needed to use the potty, and I noticed a rather large bruise or cut on his buttocks (or wherever it may be)"*.

Let them answer you. Be sure to record their answer in the file. The reason for all of this is: should there ever be a reason for concern of abuse, you want a record of what you have seen, so the blame is not put on you as the culprit.

Reporting Injuries

I am sure you have seen in the news or online over the years about the daycare center or in-home daycare provider being blamed for injuries etc., and sometimes, they are justified. If you come across a bruise or suspected child abuse situation, you have to report it to the DSS immediately. You are a mandated reporter as a daycare provider. They will instruct you on what to do, or they will take care of it themselves. Having your records of past situations, as well as current ones may be of service. Having a file on the children is not a secret.

I always informed parents at interviews that I do keep one on all children. I may refer to it in passing…." oh great! You have his immunizations; I'll just put this in **his file**" …or… "I keep records on *all* my daycare kids; it keeps things in order for me". Either way, it's your business and record-keeping is part of the business.

Digital or Paper Records

Computers are a great source to use for recordkeeping, but I have handwritten some things right on the inside of the physical file, as it is faster to access, and if you lose files on your computer, you still have a record. You can also scan physical documents into your computer if you'd like to have multiple forms of recordkeeping. If you do decide to store files on your computer, use a flash drive or Cloud/OneDrive/Dropbox website that you can access from another computer if your computer crashes.

More on this in Chapter 15: Media

Chapter 10: Preparing your Home for Daycare

Outside

Preparing your home will depend on the type of home you have. For example, if you have a split-level home, you will most likely have a deck off your top floor and possibly a patio somewhere behind the home, usually behind the garage.

GATES!!!! You will need a gate at the top of the stairs of your deck and also at the bottom. My husband built a gate placed on hinges for easy opening and closing for me with a spring-loaded lock that little ones can't open. Why at the bottom? Because if children are in the yard or patio, they can climb up the stairs and fall down the stairs. You need to keep them off the stairs. Also, the back of the stairs will need to be enclosed (no open back area, the area where your toe hits when going up). It actually makes for a nicer looking stairway and is not a place where children can either fall through while going down or up or a place for them to hang on from underneath.

Doors to garages, sheds, and buildings should not be accessible to children at any time without an adult present, so lock them with a padlock or a slide lock high out of reach. Chemicals, tools, even animals, may be stored in these areas and could cause harm or death to your children and daycare children.

If you live on a busy road/street/highway, the state will insist you fence your yard. (This is a tax deduction so keep any and all receipts for the building materials, and labor involved). You need to keep good records so it will benefit you come tax time. The fence can be the entire yard or simply the area in which the children will play in (as long as it is attached to the entrance to the yard.)

For example: if you are only fencing in the area next to the patio, the children need to be able to enter this area without crossing the area that is not fenced. Several children underfoot can take off and find themselves in the street in a hurry. Some yards that are centered in the neighborhood away from heavy traffic usually do not need to have a fenced yard. Your county DSS worker can answer this question for you as well as other requirements.

If you have a gate in your fence, this too will have to have a latch the children cannot operate to let themselves out. A self-closing latch that locks is best. Personally, I would suggest you fence in the yard. I felt the children were safer in an enclosed environment. People and dogs could make their way into a non-fenced yard which could cause an issue you don't want.

In MN, we lived on a park with soccer fields, softball fields, a skating rink, and a playground. There was a path that ran right past our home leading into the park. Because I had such an elaborate playset in our yard and we lived next to a park, when the neighborhood kids would go down the path to the playground at the park, they would run into our yard thinking they had arrived! Also, though I knew most who walked by some I did not, and I wasn't comfortable with someone being able to come that close to the daycare or my own children. We fenced soon after building and moving in because of this. This is my personal opinion regarding fencing the yard.

Playsets/Swing Sets

You will need a base of something such as pea gravel, mulch, wood chips, sand under your playset to offer a cushion in case of a fall. The thickness will also be found in your DSS packet from your state; however, a six-inch base is standard. Enclosing them with wood frameworks nicely to hold the base in place and out of your grass, I would suggest a double beam frame. We added triangle seats on each corner and the kids liked that to sit on.

Sandboxes

Don't bother unless it has a cover. Outdoor cats can make a litter box out of your sandbox and rain/leaves find their way into it as well. I would suggest white sand (which can be found at your local hardware store) because it is clean. The gray kind is usually not cleaned.

Outdoor Toys

Be sure they are quality toys and can stand up to weather if you are not using a toy box or shed. Avoid metal trucks because of rusting. Again, if you use a toy box, it must be safe, have an open area for air, and that children cannot lock themselves into. Children like to play hide and seek, climb into these, and suffocate or get overheated. NEVER allow children to play in the box and be sure it can be opened from the inside! Laundry baskets work well to hold toys and simply drill a few holes in the bottom, so they don't collect rainwater.

Being A Courteous Neighbor Who Works from Home

At the end of each day, have the children help in putting toys away in their proper place. Toys go back in the box or basket. Riding toys etc. get lined up under the slide for instance. Keeping your yard neat and tidy not only teaches children to be responsible at the end of playtime for the day, but it also shows you care about your neighbors. Your yard may be visible to neighbors through a fence, or from a second story. Be a good neighbor and clean up after the day.

This includes if you have had the kids play in the driveway at the end of the day waiting for parents to pick up. If you use your driveway for games, basketball, riding toys, etc. be sure to rope off the end of your driveway or place caution cones or signs (which can be found online or toy stores) to keep anyone from driving *into* your driveway.

I personally parked my large van at the end of the driveway on the street so that no one could drive into my driveway. This was in MN where I didn't have to have parents park in the driveway when arriving.. Parents will be thankful for your precaution. This is also a good time if playing at the end of the day, to have the children's backpacks, bags, etc. outside with them, so when parents pick them up, they can grab and go!

So, when the day is over and all kids have gone, toys should not be strewn about in front of your home or yard. Some neighborhoods actually have rules about this. Be a good neighbor and place the riding toys etc. in the garage, out of sight. If you don't do this, even if your neighborhood doesn't have any rules about this, you may make someone upset by this and they just may make a call to DSS about your daycare, and they are required to come out and investigate. If this does happen, they will be going through the home and yard as well.

Inside

There are obvious things you should do, whether doing daycare in your home or you have your own young children. Here is a list of the top twelve:

1. Cover all unused outlets with covers (they are very inexpensive and can be found at most discount stores such as Walmart or Target.

2. Only single cords should hang from any blinds, to avoid strangulation.

3. Safety latches on cabinets such as those under the kitchen and bathroom sinks, on kitchen drawers that have utensils, or plastic wraps with sharp tear-off edges on their boxes.

4. Gates at the top/bottom of stairways to keep children in designated areas.

5. Store all cleaning chemicals, perfumes, at least 3 ft up from the floor.

6. A fire extinguisher should be on every floor of your home. Although most states only require you to have one in the kitchen, I feel one for every floor is better. When we were in MN with our split-level home, the fire Marshall suggested that I keep my fire extinguisher in my front foyer closet, since that was the central area. (I had a split-level home at the time) I did that, but I still kept one under my kitchen sink and one in my downstairs laundry room.

7. First Aid Kit (relatively inexpensive and can be purchased at all drug stores, Target, Walmart, grocery stores, etc.) I would suggest one for your kitchen, children's bathroom, and your car or van for field trips, and one in the stroller for those trips to the park.

8. Ipecac (to induce vomiting) The state will require you to have a minimum of three bottles of this in your home in case of accidental poisoning. Keep this out of reach of children.

9. Remove all extension cords, the Fire Marshall will find those and site you for this. Power strips however are acceptable and are useful for stereo equipment, Christmas lights, etc.

10. Laundry Rooms/Utility Rooms need to be behind a locked door, a latch high on the door is sufficient in most cases. If you have a litter box in one of these areas, a gate can be used as well so the animal has access. Some people use cat doors cut into the door.

11. If you have a gas stove with knobs on the front of the unit, some states will require you to have a locking control so that children cannot turn on the burner. I had one that I had just purchased and had it returned for an electric stove. Another option is to simply remove the knobs during daycare hours.

12. Escape plan of home posted in a prominent place. I taped mine to the inside of my foyer closet door. This is a floor plan of your home with exits highlighted in case of fire, along with a meeting place outside the home and away from danger. The plan should also show where you would go in case of a tornado.

The Playroom

This might be 1. a room over your garage (depending on your county's regulations) 2. A garage as long as the space is free from hazards and units are out of reach. 3. A bedroom 4. A family room 5. A Dining room that isn't being used as one. Basically, what you need is a room large enough to have children play freely with toys and furniture without making things too small. Some counties will regulate specifically how large the play area must be by square feet.

Setting up the Playroom: If you have a variety of ages in your care, it can be helpful to have areas set up for those age groups. For example, I had a kitchen area with a highchair, a table and chairs, a doll bed, and a place with a shelf next to it with age-appropriate toys and books. On the other side of the bookshelf, I had a baby area. I had the sponge lock-together pieces on the floor for an added cushion. This is where I had a Sit & Play Station, (like a walker that doesn't move). I had a basket with soft toys and board books, and it was a safe place for the little ones who don't crawl yet or even the ones that do.

You have to be very aware of what is out while little ones are playing and not napping. They put everything in their mouths. This is another good reason for a place gated off for the little ones. I also at times had a reading corner. Filled with oversized pillows and baskets of books. We would all sit together for storytime.

If you have a large room, it's nice to set things up like this. If you don't, just be creative and find a way to make areas safe and fun for the different age groups. I often changed the room around over the weekend, to give it a new look and the kids loved that! They would notice right away, and everything seemed new. It's also a good idea to put some toys away and rotate them out so they don't get bored with the same toys every day.

Toys

When I started daycare, I had a young child of my own already, so I had many toys, puzzles, and riding toys. If you are starting a daycare with no children of your own, I would suggest hitting every garage sale that lists "kid's toys" and watch for ads of "daycare closing". There are many sale sites now through Facebook that weren't even a thing when I started mine, but that is a great place to find things, and sometimes even for free!

Toys can be very expensive so be selective on brands. Some are known for their durability, such as Step II, Fisher-Price, V-Tech. They are also known for holding their color. Young children's' toys are usually in good condition and can be had for a fraction of the cost.

You will want a variety of age-appropriate toys. Duplicates of toys/ puzzles, balls, barbie dolls, baby dolls, trucks, matchbox cars, etc. are needed. There needs to be enough for children within each age group to have access to toys. If there is only one baby doll and there are 3-4 kids in the age group that would play with that doll, it's important to have several baby dolls.

You will also need toys that work on small motor skills, such as Legos, building blocks, puzzles. Also, large motor skills such as climbing gyms, tunnels, basketball. Mind provoking toys such as puzzles, games, memory games, computer games, tablets, Leapfrog, etc... Nurturing toys such as stuffed toys and baby dolls.

After-School Kids Toys

Older children will need stimulating toys such as beads for stringing necklaces, board games, decks of cards, computer games, books, etc.

Chapter 11: Equipment

Cribs for babies:

You will need an approved crib. Don't buy cribs at garage sales unless they can supply a receipt that shows it was manufactured within the last 5 years. Codes change frequently regarding cribs and safety is incredibly important. Target, Walmart, etc., have great portable cribs. You do not need a full-size crib. They fold easily for storing away and the mattress slides into the crib as well for storage. They are reasonably priced under $100. Don't bother with bumper pads or mobiles, they are prohibited, due to strangulation or suffocation. If you want something cute and practical, invest in a lighted globe that shows stars, etc. on the ceiling that rotates to soothe the baby.

All you need are a few fitted sheets and a lightweight blanket. I used a loosely crocheted blanket because crochet blankets have holes that allow airflow and prevent suffocation. Do NOT use pillows or stuffed animals in cribs until the child is at least 18 months old. SIDS has been associated with pillows and soft crib toys. A teething ring or light blanket would be fine.

I also elevated the side of the crib where the baby's head was. I just feel there is so much information out there about SIDS and respiratory issues associated that if the mattress is elevated on one end it will help the child's breathing. I did this for my own children, and I did this for my daycare kids.

Meshed Sided Portable Cribs (Pack-N-Play)

They are a great way to keep the young ones safe while in the playroom or other areas, such as outside in the play area. However, while I was doing daycare still in 2016 the state of SC outlawed using these for napping in. I am sure there was an issue that prompted this new law. The sale sites were loaded with daycares selling these as they now had to buy the portable cribs. This was surely an added expense for all the daycares. I saved two of mine and sold two. I bought an additional portable crib, so I now had two cribs, and two pack n plays. Once a child is two years old, they do not need to be in a crib for nap times.

Strollers

Don't bother with a single stroller unless you intend to only have one child under the age of 4. The cost of a double stroller isn't much more and will save you on children too tired to walk and added storage for outings. They fold up as easily as a single stroller and most stores such as Target, etc. will have a great selection, along with garage/yard sales, and consignment shops too. Even though it's a double stroller, I could easily fit three kids in. One in front and two in the back with the back support folded back some if not all the way. And believe me, walking back to the house after playing hard at the park, you will have one or two kids complain they are tired and don't want to walk.

Walkers/Stations

Walkers are not looked at as a safe thing for the pre-walker in daycare, though they weren't outlawed. I remember years ago, I had only one little one on the verge of walking. We were in the front on the driveway, so the kids could play basketball, skateboard, draw with chalk, and use riding toys. There was literally nothing for this little guy to do, so I brought out the walker and connected a dog's long leash on it and attached it to my garage door rail. It was perfect and he could walk all over the driveway and play with the kids. A few years later I purchased a station that allowed them to swivel, but they couldn't move the station. There are many things attached to entertain them in the station. They do take up a lot of room, so keep that in mind if you decide to purchase one of these. But they are great for keeping a baby entertained when they're just on the verge of walking.

Infant Toys

There are a variety of floor toys for babies. Colorful large, quilted blankets with A-Framed toys that sit over the top of the baby laying on the quilt with small toys attached hanging down towards the baby. If you have a baby on the floor, be right next to them in case of spit-up and also if they are having tummy time.

Infant/Toddler and Preschool Car Seats

Only if you have proper car seats for your daycare children as well as your own if you *ever* consider traveling with the children. Babies need to be facing the rear in an infant carrier until they are at least 1 year in most states. The base will be secured with the belt and latching square to be sure it is secure, and the infants' carrier will snap into place. Be sure to research the car seat height or weight requirements for each of the children in your care if you plan to travel with them!

Chapter 12: Safety

Cell Phones

Always have a cell phone if you go on field trips or even a walk to the neighborhood park. For safety reasons as well as something as unexpected as getting caught in traffic or a parent calls to say they are picking up early and you aren't at home. I had that happen one time. I was late getting back, and a couple of parents were in my driveway. I explained I forgot my phone and apologized, and they were fine since it was only about 15 minutes. I never let that happen again. Keep all parent's phone numbers in your phone, including their work number. Your cellphone is a tax-deductible expense.

Emergency Cards

Although not required, it is a good idea to have a card with important information on each child along with their photo. You may never have to use this, but if you do, it would be of great service.

T-shirts

I bought about 15 neon green t-shirts in a variety of sizes. I had my daycare's name stenciled on them. "Tam's Kids" I also had a number on them. Now I wish I hadn't done the numbers because the kids would actually argue who got to wear for example the one with the number 4 on it because I had several kids who were 4. I did it because I thought it was cute and like a sports jersey style. What was great, however, was my daycare kids were easy to see on a crowded playground. I would count the kids about once a minute while pushing one on a swing or catching one on a slide, or simply sitting on the bench watching them. The kids looked adorable and I was always told by other parents on our outings "what a great idea!" it's also great free advertising!

Chapter 13: So... Who Pays for Stuff?

Diapers

You do not pay for these items. Have the parents supply you either daily or with a lot to be kept at your home until they need to be replenished. If a parent asks you to supply these, I would simply say that is not considered in the rate for daycare and you would have to charge him/her for that plus your travel time. I would not however agree to reimbursement should you choose to do this. Figure how many are needed each week, the cost of this, and add to your weekly rate along with your time for travel to buy them. Or, you simply say you do not supply diapers and they need to be sure their child has them in their bag. The other issue with you purchasing them is that each family uses a different brand or a specific size and keeping track of those brands/sizes for each child to go and purchase each time would be difficult.

Pull-Ups

Same as above. They supply those for their children. Have them label them with their child's name on the package.

Wet Wipes

Same with wet wipes. I put the child's name on the wet wipes. I did keep a box of wet wipes on hand in case I ran out. And I did keep a package of diapers as well just in case.

Cloth Diapers

I did not accept those. I had parents ask during interviews and I said *"as much as I appreciate that you want to use those, I ask that you do not use them here. I do not want to "store" them, even if they offer to bring a Diaper Genie. I do not want soiled diapers left in my home even if in a container."* It's usually first-time parents that will ask about this.

Sunscreen

This is expensive. Because it is applied several times a day when playing outside, it is important that each child has their own with their name on it. I had an inground pool. Because of that, I insisted on no lotion sunscreen. It must be a sport spray type, which I prefer rather than rubbing on each child. The lotion type really messed with my pool clarity. When I would run out of sunscreen, I would send a text message to the parent as well as a note in their daily bag to replenish. I made it clear to the parents that the children will not be sharing sunscreen and to be sure your child has a supply so they can play in the pool and outside with the others.

Storage

I had an under the stairs closet off my kitchen. On my door and inside, I had shelves for storage. I kept a row of diapers/pull-ups for each child. I also kept the sunscreen for each child on another shelf. A basket on another shelf with their swimsuit that was kept at my home. I laundered them once a week or more if needed.

They also kept one beach towel at my home, which I also laundered once a week or more if needed. If the child has only one bathing suit, they sometimes want to take home on weekends, that is fine, but you need to remind parents to bring the suit back on Monday. I encouraged parents, if they could, to bring more than one bathing suit. It is so easy for parents to forget to bring things and without a swimsuit, the kids couldn't go in the pool. For this reason, I also had a couple of extra pairs of swimsuits.

Baby's Milk/Formula

In my daycare, I let the parents know up front that if they are breast-feeding to bring me a frozen bank of milk or daily amounts needed, and one container of formula as a backup. I asked for it to be already in the bottles so as to not come in contact with the breast milk. Or if they bring it in bags, I would wear latex gloves when handling breast milk. If they are formula fed, I ask that they supply that as well. Baby formula is expensive, and I wouldn't want that added expense.

If you are on the state provided food program, they may tell you that you can't make the parent pay for the formula. So, the way I handled that was: I told the parents, I will charge you this much a week for daycare if I supply the formula to cover my costs of travel to get it, etc. No one ever did that. They brought the formula. I also told them I do not supply baby food. You can't claim it on most food programs, so it doesn't make sense to buy it.

I told my parents that they can supply that as well when the child reaches that age of baby food. I also offered to run the food I am serving the older kids through a food processor for the baby, but that was back when I supplied lunch. I stopped that in the latter half of my years of doing daycare. I did suggest that if the parents wanted to supply me with frozen baby food that I would keep it and let them know when it needed replenishing. I did this for my own kids. If I was making peas, for example, I would run them through the food processor and then pour into ice cube trays and freeze them. Then I could take it out as needed, thaw and heat it up and I wasn't serving processed food.

Tissues

During seasons of colds, I will ask if anyone could donate some tissues for daycare. Most parents will do this. When you have several kids with runny noses, it goes fast. Request the kind with lotion so noses don't get sore. Don't feel embarrassed asking for this. Schools and church daycare centers do all the time.

Chapter 14: To Provide or Not to Provide Food...

As I mentioned earlier, I discontinued serving breakfast first and then later also discontinued lunch. I only kept providing afternoon snack time. The following are the reasons for both.

Breakfast

I was serving breakfast to my own kids and thought it wasn't a big deal as I had some early daycare kids. However, it was killing my food budget and also gave me more of a mess to pick up after as I still had lunch and snack time. I felt like I was constantly cleaning up in the kitchen. So, I asked parents to have their children already fed if they arrived after 8 a.m. And if they came before that, they would need to bring something for their child to have to eat if they hadn't already done so at home. Most fed them at home after that, but a few would bring a snack bar and juice box. So that wasn't a big deal as far as I was concerned.

Lunch

I was about ten years into doing daycare when I came to the decision to discontinue providing lunch. It started one summer. I had a full daycare and making lunch for that many kids was really expensive and there were several that would waste food or tell me "my mom says I don't have to eat that, or everything, etc." So, I sent home a note to all parents stating that I had a large waste of food going on at lunchtime. I also pointed out that since we spend a lot of time in the pool in the summers and eat outside at the tables poolside, it would be a big help if they could pack a picnic-style lunch for their child of things they knew they liked.

"Picnic style" lunch means, something I am *not* heating up. It means juice boxes or water bottles with the water *already* in it. Simply put, the type of lunch they would send with a school-age child. Otherwise, if each child grabs their lunch box/bag and we all head outside and get settled at our table... and Johnny says *"my mom needs you to heat up my spaghetti O's"*... well, that means everyone has to come back inside with me because I can't leave them out there by themselves.

I had no problem helping them with straws in the juice boxes or opening their Lunchables, etc. I just needed the food to be ready for eating when we all got outside.

This was a huge success. It really gave me less to clean up, it helped with my food budget, and the stress of planning lunches was gone. The kids were eating what *they* liked and there was less food waste. It was so nice that in the fall, I sent home a note letting parents know that this was such a success for all the above reasons and in lieu of raising rates this year, I am eliminating providing lunch. There was not one complaint.

Because I made this decision, I was able to provide better/healthier snacks for the afternoon, though not daily. If we went on an outing to the park, I would always bring snack bars and juice boxes/water for halfway through the morning.

Food Programs

What is the food program? It is a state-funded program to ensure that children are given a balanced diet for meals and snacks. For some children, it may be their only really good meal they get for the day. They send you a check each month for payment of such.

> ***Example:*** If I feed 6 children lunch and snack every day for a week, I record that. I also record what exactly they ate. Not how much, but what I served. The state then puts a value on it.
>
> For instance, snacks .15 lunch .80 (rates will be different, this is from approximately 2002.) At the end of the month, you turn in your record of who ate, what they ate, when they ate, and what days they ate it. Then they send you a check the following month.

Each state is different, as are their tiers for your area or family situations. The Food Program person will come to your house at least once a year on a scheduled visit and at least once a year unannounced. They will come during a mealtime or snack time. They will count heads and ask the kids questions, such as "what did you have for lunch today? Did everyone wash his or her hands before eating?"

They will check your records of each daily menu that must be kept current daily! They will check your fridge to be sure everything has a cover, and that it is clean. They will write up a report on you, give you more forms if you need them, and leave until the next time.

It may sound a little scary, but I actually had a really great Program Lady, and she was so nice and very realistic. They may not all be like mine though. There was a time this program could really help with the food budget. But over the years, the rates per meal and snack dropped so low that I discontinued it. To me, it wasn't worth the paperwork and the unannounced visits and scheduled visits. If you don't mind the paperwork, it will be just fine for you.

Chapter 15: Media

Reminder Notices, Information Sheets, Newsletters, & Daycare Facebook pages:

These are great ways to keep parents up to date on happenings! I was very big on multiple forms of communication because things get busy at drop off and pick-up times, and you may think you will remember to tell BillyBob's mom to bring more diapers, or Sarah's dad to remember to pick up on time, but sometimes you will forget and depending on what the communication is that could be a problem.

I started out doing a newsletter each week. I put so much time and love into this and would pack it into their Friday Folders (or whatever their last day of the week is for them) that went home with them. I scanned in photos and wrote cute little things the kids said or did that week. I had reminders, fun things coming up, announcements of a field trip, reminders not to forget to send in the admission money for their child, a vacation time I may be taking, or asking them to let me know when they will take their vacations so I knew what each week would like, especially in the summer or during school breaks or holiday breaks. I posted pictures of the kids working on their crafts, etc. The parents LOVED it. It was a great tool for both parents to see since we all know mom and dad don't always communicate on everything!

Then along came Facebook! With the help of my son, we created a private Facebook group just for my daycare families. No one else can access it. What a great way to share information and pictures of the kids! And I could upload videos of the kids, which is very nice for the parents. I even used it for things I was asking for in donations like construction paper for crafts. If I had something to sell, or my families were selling something, they could post on there as well. It was a great tool, and I strongly suggest you implement that into your daycare. It's also eco-friendly, no paper, no ink!

I also had a public Facebook page advertising my daycare. So those permission forms are important here so that I could share pictures of the kids or have a group photo as my header.

Chapter 16: A Family-Friendly Home

This can be a challenge depending on how organized you are. If you have a playroom where all the toys and projects are done, you can close the door at the end of the day and go about your family life if you don't want your home to look like a daycare setting.

Personally, even though this was my profession for 21 years, I wanted to enjoy my home as my home when the day was done. After all, I was there 24/7 and I don't want to feel like I'm still at work when it's 5 p.m. or the weekend.

So here are a few ideas to help keep work separate from home:
- Highchairs can be a big space taker. Graco is one company that makes a collapsible chair that hooks right onto your breakfast bar or table. They are great because they have a snap-on tray, safety belts, they lock in place, but best yet, they fold up and can be stored away and out of sight. I used bar stools for my older kids along with my kitchen table when needed.

- That closet under the stairs I talked about earlier also had hooks on the wall. I could fold up the highchairs and hang on those at the end of the day. If I used a toddler table and chairs, which I did at times, this also can be folded and placed in the closet along the wall along with the chairs folded up.

- I already explained how I stored diapers/pull-ups, etc. on the racks and shelving in that same closet.

- The beach towels the kids brought were kept in my pool shed, folded on the shelf. Each child knew exactly which towel was there, and I have to say, with all the beach towels with characters on them (little mermaid, cars, stripes, etc.) there were never two of the same! When we were done with the pool, the kids would hang their towels on my fence to dry and their bathing suits were laid out on the plastic kid's tables by my pool to dry.

- I had a decorative basket in my family room that I kept small children's toys in. This was to entertain them while waiting for all kids to arrive in the early mornings. They would go back to the basket when all arrived, and we were now in the playroom or outside.

With all of these storage tricks...there was no sign that I did daycare when you walked into my house after hours unless you went to the playroom upstairs. All toys outside were placed in the toybox and riding toys were neatly put in a row under the slide. Pool toys were placed in the toy bin along with life jackets. Floaters would be stacked next to the toybox in the backyard by the pool. The kids knew what was expected of them, and they had no issue putting things away. If mom or dad showed up early, I still expected them to take care of their own things, and mom and dad would wait a short time for this to happen.

This was just another part of daycare, teaching the kids how to put things away and tidy up when they are done playing. Without making this a part of the curriculum, I would've been putting an enormous cleanup task on myself and my children - which isn't fair. Plus, it is a disservice to the daycare children not to teach them these life skills. Make your life easier and teach children how to tidy up!

Winter

If you live in a state where there is winter, as I did when I was doing daycare in MN for many years of my daycare career you need a plan so daycare winter items don't take over your home. Winter presents a problem with extra coats, snow pants, boots, shoes, hats, mittens, etc. I came up with a solution that worked well for me and can be used at any time of the year.

I had a service door to my garage as one walked up the front walk. Because the front door could sometimes be a wind tunnel, (could literally take my storm door off the hinges) I had families enter my home through the garage service door. The families entered my home through the garage. I had a sign on the door before going in that said, "Please carry your snow boots in and place them in the downstairs closet along with your things." If I didn't, my carpeted stairs would have been a dirty mess in no time.

They would go down the few steps to my lower level and at the bottom, I had a large closet that went under the stairs but large and tall enough to walk into it. Along the wall I had hooks placed and above the hooks, the child's name typed and taped to the wall. Below the hook was a snow tray for their boots. *They would hang their coats and snow pants there and stuff their hat and mittens into the boots in the tray. If they had a backpack or bag it sat along the opposite wall. This kept the mess out of my house, which could also be something to trip over.

When we came inside from playing in the snow, each child knew where to hang their pants and coats so they could dry out and where to put their boots. Some children kept their extra snow pants at my house so they didn't have to bring those every day and would take them home on Fridays. Or they had an extra pair they simply kept at my home. Some kids even kept their boots at my house as well. I always offered that to the parents so that wouldn't be an issue if they were forgotten at home and we were going to be playing out in the snow that day. I kept a drawer with extra hats and mittens for the child who forgot theirs.

Summer

Since my daycare families entered my home through the garage, I had a long wall that led to the door that entered my home. Our garage was a 2½ car garage, and we had the garage door *offset* to allow for a workbench and walkway. I had the same setup with the hooks, and names, etc. for them there. It made it very easy for drop-off and pick-up times to have all their things easy for the parents to access. *I didn't use *this* area in the winter because I didn't want to send the kids home with cold coats and boots to put on. My garage was not heated.

I had an area under some shelving in the garage that housed the riding toys, a box of basketballs, bouncing balls, etc. that the kids used if we happened to be playing in the front. We did that sometimes close to pick up time.

Footwear:
I asked that parents do not send their children in sandals that have buckles. They are difficult, and it's nice if kids can put their shoes on, so either slip-on or Velcro straps are preferred.

Clothes for babies:
I asked that they are in "diaper changing friendly" clothes. I need something easy to take off and put back on. Snaps can be fussy. Regarding clothes for Potty Training kids: I asked for easy to pull up and pull-down pants/shorts. No belts. No ties. We want them to be successful.

The Playroom

The playroom in my first home was a guest bedroom converted. I had shelves with toys and colorful walls. I painted a large rainbow and a pot of gold which turned out nicely. I had the night sky on one wall with the moon and stars. I had plastic bins for soft toys, baskets with dolls, and bins with more toys/books. I had a small kitchen set and a child's size round table and chairs. All purchased at garage sales. I even had room for a small plastic picnic table in the room. My daycare was new, and I only had a few kids, so it worked out well, plus I had my daughter who was only one year old at the time. At the end of the day, I could close the door if I wanted and leave work behind.

In my second home, I also used a large guest bedroom for my playroom, but since we had the house built, we didn't finish off that room. Instead, we hung sheetrock and left the floor cement. I bought large, finished edge area rugs at Home Depot and placed them next to each other. My thought was, if anyone spills anything, it's not a big deal. If someone takes a crayon or marker to the wall, it's also not a big deal. But what we did was hang our artwork and drawings on the unfinished walls. I had the ABC's/Numbers that ribboned across the top part of the wall all around the room. I also hung colorful curtains and bought large learning posters from Hobby Lobby in the teacher section. I had posters like animals, fish, ocean life, colors, and the word for each color, etc. We had a special area on the wall for our most recent artwork. After a couple of weeks, the kids would take those home and they were replaced with our new artwork!

When buying storage bins, I would suggest clear ones so the kids can see what goes in there. Most won't be able to read so you either tape a picture of what goes in the bin or have it clear so they can see what goes where. Plastic three drawer bins on wheels are great, especially if you like to change the room around once in a while. By the way, the kids love it when you do this. They get all excited when things look different and new.

Sleeping Mats are great and take little room to store versus cots. They are still the same as they were from kindergarten. They trifold up for easy storage as well. Spend the extra money and get the thicker one, it's more comfortable. Each child needs to have their OWN pillow and blanket that is kept in a bin just for them and have their name on the bin.

In the kitchen (my kitchen), I have one cabinet dedicated to daycare plastic dishes. If you are serving food or even if they bring their own food, sometimes they might need a plate. I bought the ones with dividers. It's easier for them to scoop up their food and keep food separate since kids tend to not like food to touch anyway. I also used paper plates and cups when I felt a need to have things be simple.

I also had a large family room down the hallway, and we hung out there as well, to watch videos, spread out with large blocks, even to play children's games on the computer.

Pets/Animals

All animals (domesticated or farm) must be up to date on their shots and be registered with your city and or county. This will be checked by your DSS provider. If you have a dog that is not safe to be around children, that animal must be kept separate from the children at all times. Dogs must be kept out of the area of children eating at all times, whether in another room or behind a gate.

Chapter 17: Preschool Programs

This is what sets you apart from any other home daycares. Having a preschool program in your daycare! You don't have to have a teaching license to teach children the basics in your home.

There are many programs to choose from and once you are licensed with the county, you will begin receiving mail from different companies and online selling their programs. I used the "affordable Preschool Program" throughout the years along with some others.

I offered my program to age 2½ and older. You will get a monthly packet full of crafts, projects, science experiments, cooking, ABCs, counting, etc. all done in an easy-to-follow way. All materials are usually included in most programs. If you offer to do projects from a program 3-4 days a week for a couple of hours each, your daycare will stand out from the other daycare interviews they've been to. With Pinterest and other online crafts to look up, if you have the imagination, you can create some of your own crafts for the children.

I almost always had an infant or a young one in my daycare. While they took their morning nap, I would do my preschool program. This way you can devote your attention to the older children and have your monitor near you so you can hear if one of the young ones wakes up. By the time we were done with our crafts and learning time, naps were over, and it was time for lunch. This also helps make the day move along and have some routine.

Schedule Routine

Routine is the key. Children thrive with routine. Not so strict that there isn't room for something new, but to have a fairly good routine is key. If I have a toddler that isn't taking a morning nap because that one has been eliminated from their schedule, I will give them something to do along with the older kids. Some markers/crayons and paper usually work nicely.

I had a routine for my week, and you will develop one too. One that works well for you. I took advantage of my afternoons, a.k.a. 'naptime' to have a little time for myself. I had my lunch at that time, I might watch a recorded show, or read the paper while I eat. Stay up to date with life outside of your daycare world. It's easy to stay locked in the world of daycare. It's important to your well-being to be informed on life within your town, city, and worldwide. I always enjoyed little chats with certain daycare parents at pick-up time. While standing outside and the kids are playing on the playset, many times the parent also wants a moment or two to engage in conversation while watching their child interact with the other kids. An adult conversation may very well be something that becomes very important to you.

I may also use my afternoon naptime to throw in some laundry, maybe check on my dinner in the crockpot that was prepared in the morning. Since naptime is approximately 2-2½ hours, you have plenty of time to do things around the house, or simply relax. I did a bit of both. I found a lot of pleasure in knowing I had things done around the house.

Cleaning Routine

Since you work from home, you are there 24/7. I made it a priority to have my household chores done by Friday afternoon, so I could enjoy my home, my family during the weekend. That was something I liked doing. On Thursdays, I would clean bathrooms not used by the kids and change my children's bed linens. I always washed my floors on Friday afternoons, changed my bed linens, and the bathroom the kids use would be cleaned.

Because I don't clean the bathroom the kids use until Friday afternoons, I would take all the toys that end up in young one's mouths and throw them in the bathtub to be cleaned. And I would wipe down toys that couldn't be submerged in water. Once the kids are all gone on Friday, I would clean the fingerprints from my front glass/screen door along with my dog's nose smudges. I would gather all pillowcases and naptime blankets and throw them in the wash. Vacuum the Playroom and hallways. Keeping things clean is important to a daycare to keep germs at bay.

Now my weekend could begin! and I had a clean house and nothing to keep me from my own family time. This worked for my family, you may very well have a different take on this.

There were always two cleanup times. One in the morning before lunch and one close to the end of the day, so that all was back in order. Each child was given a job (for example, John and Sally are going to pick up all the blocks and cars). Ben and Julie will pick up all the play kitchen items and put all dolls away. If we had a craft, all kids were expected to pick up anything that made it to the floor, such as paper, sequins, etc. I never just said, "ok let's clean up". They need to have a 'job' to do, or they just wander. This helps them to learn to compartmentalize little jobs for clean-up.

Arts and Crafts

On days we do messy things such as finger painting, when we finished, I would have the children walk across the hall to my laundry room. I had a step stool set by the utility sink, and the children would take turns washing their hands, keeping the mess from my bathroom or kitchen. They had plastic art smocks so those would come off and be left in the utility sink for me to clean up later.

You will need to stock up on these basic things for your preschool/craft time:

- Construction Paper
- Scissors
- Tape
- Glue bottle
- Glue Sticks
- Glitter
- Paints
- Finger Paints and Finger Paint Paper
- Markers (washable)
- Art Smocks or dad's shirt (smocks are nice because they are colorful, the kids love them, and they are easy to wash off.)
- Buttons
- Popsicle Sticks

**Your local Costco or Sam's Club is a great place to find deals. You can get a discounted membership by owning your own business as a Daycare!

Also, don't be afraid to ask for donations from parents. Parents can be a bit competitive. For example, I would put in my daycare Facebook page that I need construction paper or sequins, and whether anyone has some they would like to donate to our craft time. Things will come flooding in along with many things not even asked for that would be great for crafts. Let them help you. I made sure to give a big shout out on the Facebook page of the families who helped out. They love recognition and it will improve your next request. *Example: "A big thank you goes to Johnny's family for sending in a bag filled with...."* Plus, I would send a personal thank you note home in their child's folder.

You never want a family's kind generosity to go without a thank you. They are helping their own child for sure, but they are also helping the other kids and you as well financially.

Friday Folders

The folder could be a Thursday or Wednesday as well depending on the child's last day for the week. On one side of the folder in the pocket are all the pictures or crafts their child has made throughout the week, and in the other pocket is the Newsletter or Reminder Notices if you feel the Facebook page isn't enough.

I wrote the child's name in large bold letters on the front of the folder. It's a big deal for the child to see their name on it. They love to share their artwork with mom and dad. If we make something too big to fit into the folder, I simply laid it on top of the folder, and mom and dad know to take this along with them.

My dining room was near the front door, and I had a large table so I would lay each folder out with their large project. I did this when there was more than a folder to take. Normally I would tuck the folder into their daily bag.

Now, some kids get so excited to show their parents what is in their folders, but I encourage the parents to have the children show this *at home* for a couple of reasons:
1) They will spill *everything* out on the floor and there is more commotion, which delays leaving and I can't be present for leaving and present for the kids still there,
2) This should be a child/parent's sharing time in their own home, and
3) It's also time for them to leave, so you can get back to the other kids.

Encourage parents to share info in those folders as well. Vacation dates, late arrivals due to doctor appointments, and thank you notes can go in the folder as well.

Chapter 18: Birthdays and Holidays

Birthdays

It is always nice to celebrate the daycare child's birthday. I would make brownies or cookies and a single birthday candle at lunchtime or snack time. We would sing happy birthday to our star, and everyone has a treat. I also would make a crown out of construction paper for them to wear at lunchtime and snack time and of course on their way home. It would have their name, their new age, and decorations.

I discourage parents from bringing in cupcakes. They want to bring them, but I explain that all the kids do is eat the frosting and the cake ends up all over my floor. It's just extra work for me. I explain I will happily give them brownies or cookies or ice cream cups.

Also, I did NOT allow latex balloons. They are a choking hazard. A child can bite it and the latex goes deep into the throat and the child can die. Mylar balloons are fine.

Tips and Tricks

I keep a box of gifts on hand for birthdays, special occasions, etc. I gave an age-appropriate gift. Watch for sales at the stores. I could pick up gifts like Barbies or toy trucks, a packet of matchbox cars, etc. for less than $5. I rarely spent more than that. Even the young ones get something such as a stuffed animal, for example.

When you see a good deal, take advantage of that, and put it away for these occasions. One year I found beautiful angel ornaments and gave those to the little girls born around Christmas time for their birthdays. There will be times when you've forgotten a birthday and you'll be very glad you have a stash of gifts on hand to pull from.

I look all year for Christmas gifts. For both the kids and the parents. LTD Magazine is a good source as well. Parents trust me with their children and pay my salary so I will always find something awesome for them. All the parents will get the same kind of gift. Of course, it changes each year, and I keep a record of that, so I don't duplicate!

Examples of different years for the parents were: One year each got a set of stem wine glass/stemless wine glasses or low-ball drink glasses. Another year each got a large box of beautiful Christmas ornaments. All different designs but the same amount or close to it. Another year: Christmas hand towels and a candle that coordinated with the towels. Another year: Christmas table runners.

Now, I look for all these the day after Christmas! That is when the best assortment is available, and you can get them so much cheaper for the next year. I think of how many families I have in my daycare and I decide what I can get that will be the right number of gifts that I can get that is somewhat similar for all the families. I will usually buy one or two more just in case I have more families the next year.

You can do address books, journals, or stationery sets as a theme--that way no one knows what they are getting when they open theirs at the Christmas party, which we get into later. I try to keep it to about $8-$10 with the discount after Christmas you are getting something worth much more for so much less!

Pack these away with your Christmas decorations. I had a Rubbermaid bin marked daycare Christmas gifts. I won't deny, sometimes I had a family that I had grown very close with and I sometimes gave them a little extra gift on the side. I still have lifelong friends of families I did daycare for. As mentioned previously

I also look for gifts for the children, if I don't already have a good stock. I buy kid footballs, trucks, Barbies, baby dolls, matchbox cars, For the kid's gift, I will try to keep it at about $8-$10 each and if you shop wisely you can do it. That's why I am always looking throughout the year as well.

Christmas break

I didn't do this the first couple years of my daycare, however, When I met my neighbor after we built a new home who was also a daycare provider and she showed me how important it is to take a break, be with your own family, and recharge so to speak. I didn't have any issues with parents about me taking this break, except for two fathers that I recall.

> **STORYTIME!**
>
> The first father told me he didn't realize I needed "a break from babysitting". I explained to him the difference between a babysitter and a daycare provider i.e., daily care, is that a daycare provider works anywhere from 8-10 hours a day. Daycare includes a preschool program, potty training, nurturing, field trips, swim lessons in my pool, for example. I also pointed out that if he broke down what I actually made per hour from his family, it came to about $2.20 per hour. Whereas at the time the going rate for a babysitter was approximately $9.00-$10.00 per hour and typically their services are pretty basic and only for a few hours. I replied that I would be happy to be referred to as a babysitter as long as I was paid those rates as well. He understood.
>
> The second father couldn't understand why I needed to take a break and also be paid for it. Whether it was for Christmas or any vacation time I took. I explained that the Friday folders represent only a small part of my time with his children, but it did show that I was educating them. With that comes a lot of energy and prep time. I pointed out the field trips and time teaching his children to swim in my pool. I pointed out the constant upkeep of having an in-home daycare so that my home is not only presentable for my family but also for my daycare, which meant constant cleaning. As well as potty training his son, etc. I asked him if when he took his family to the beach that past summer if he still received his paycheck, which of course he replied yes, he did. So, I explained, when I take time off, I too need to know I have paid time off which of course was discussed at interview time when I made a point of saying I am paid 52 weeks a year, no exceptions. I count on a certain income as I too have a mortgage and bills. I also explained which I feel was the most important of all is that I need to recharge. I need mom time with my own family. I want to be the best I can be for his family and the other kids and to do that I need my PTO as well. A happy and rested Daycare Provider is a

> productive and patient-provider. He completely understood after my explanation and we were good from then on.

Never apologize for needing time off. You work hard. My hours a week were 52½ hours, 7 AM to 5:30 PM. I had my lunch break when the kids took a nap, but if there were kids who were older and didn't nap in the afternoon, I didn't really get a break. And my lunchtime could be interrupted by a baby with a soiled diaper, or a child who just can't settle. You deserve time off with pay, period.

Christmas/Holiday Party

I would go out with a bang! There would be a Christmas Party that went from about 4 p.m. to 6 p.m. at the latest, and then there would be a break. For many years I had access to elaborate costumes and props from our church for the nativity scene. I would dress the kids up as the holy family, the shepherds, angels, and if we had a baby, we had baby Jesus! If not, I had a doll I used in the manger. The kids had small speaking roles as they would come out and stand in front of my Christmas tree. When all were present, they would sing some songs.

The parents and grandparents who came loved it! Lots of pictures and videos are taken. We also had years where we sang the 12 days of Christmas and the kids had posters of each that they would hold up when we got to their number, they wore Santa hats and had jingle bells and sang. Again, a big hit.

Afterward, I had lots of food and beverages for everyone. Every year the kids would get gifts for everyone, and I found that this was first of all very expensive for everyone, and not all parents would remember or participate, so I changed it. The kids would draw names so they had a gift for *one* of their playmates, and they would also have a gift for their parents, usually something pretty nice they had made during craft time. I also had gifts for all the kids and their parents.

Sometimes one of the families had an older child who would come to daycare when school was out or over the summer and I would have something for them as well. It is the only time they were *all* together with their parents and it was always a good time.

One year I was short on money for gifts, so I had a small gift for the parents, and I made up a cute coupon of a free Saturday in January they could bring their child for daycare so they could have a Saturday afternoon to themselves. Now there was only ONE Saturday offered, so it would be one and done, use it or lose it!   One year I did do a BBQ poolside for the Daycare families and that was fun too.

STORYTIME!

One year I bought all the girls in daycare a popular teen doll. If they were brunette, I gave them a brunette doll and so on. One child, when opening her gift shouted "I already have this and threw it across the room. The mom didn't do anything but say it was a nice gift and the child threw it again when mom handed it to her. There was no apology made to me by the parent or child.   This particular year, I had our Christmas party early because of everyone's schedules I believe with the school break and I had to do daycare the following day before beginning my break. Never did *that* again.

So, the following day when the child came to daycare and was sitting at my counter having her breakfast she brought, I asked her if she had anything to say to me about what happened the day before at the party. She very boldly said "Nope"! I then stopped getting her breakfast ready and got her attention and asked again. I told her that her behavior was not nice. And that I try hard to get nice things for my daycare kids and she should tell me she is sorry for behaving that way because it hurt my feelings. She simply stared at me with no intent to apologize. I explained that I don't have to get gifts for the kids, but I like to, and even if the gift isn't exactly what you would have liked it is important to be polite. She said in a very snotty tone "I'm sorry".

When they returned from Christmas break, I was asked by the mom if I had made her child apologize for what happened at the Christmas party. I told her I had. I explained exactly what I had said. I also told her I was surprised *she* hadn't insisted on it herself. I also told her since she wasn't going to use this situation as a teaching moment, that I was. I explained I don't only take care of your child, I teach the kids manners, I teach them empathy. And her child needed to be educated on both of those issues.   She was a bit embarrassed, never apologized, and left for work.   Guess mom needing a teaching moment as well.

When the party's over, the kids gather their gifts from me, and their daycare friend and they leave with their family. It's a great way to end the year and you get a much-deserved break and everyone is happy with gifts and the season. My families looked forward to this every year.

My Christmas break was always for sure December 24 through January 1. However, if the 24th fell early in the week, I would take that Monday and Tuesday for example as a paid vacation day if I had any available, which I almost always did. So that is how you determine when your last day is, to schedule your Christmas party.

Now you may be asking yourself, how many PTO days should you designate? Here's the breakdown:

1) **Two weeks Paid Time Off (PTO)**
   - **My formula (typical of most companies)**
   - PTO aka VBR is accrued at 1.6680/month for a total of 20 days of paid time off each year.
   - 10 days of PTO and 10 days PTO paid for Sick/Personal Days.

Examples of a Family who has been with you for 11 months and are leaving.
    At 11 months you have accrued 18.348 days of Paid Time Off (PTO)
    They paid you a deposit of $250.00 and they pay you $125/week.

Example 1 without any VBR used:

11 months earned 18.348 days of Paid Time Off. @ $25/day =	$458.70
No VBR was used during the 11 months (not a good idea)	$ 0.00
Deposit paid (two weeks @ $125.00 per week)	- $250.00
Balance still owed to you for VBR *not* used:	**$208.70**

Example 2 with VBR used:

11 months earned 18.348 days of Paid Time Off @ $25/day =	$458.70
Used 5 days VBR @ $25 / day	- $125.00
Balance of VBR *not* used	$333.70
Deposit paid (two weeks @ $125.00 per week)	- $250.00
Balance still owed to you VBR not used:	**$ 83.70**

First of all, I rarely used my Personal/Sick Days. But you do have them available and you have earned those. I would use them wisely. I used them if I was absolutely too ill, or upon the death of each of my parents who were in MN when I was SC. The fact that you have time earned off each month should be included in your Program Policy Booklet with the formula.

Also, this is a very good example for the Daycare Families to understand that it is good if you use your earned time off. Obviously, you will have your own set of rates and they may be higher or lower, but the formula is the same.

***A sample letter to one of my families is included with Forms at the end of this book for you to use as a template when that time comes to submit that to them.*

2) **All Major Holidays** (list each holiday in your Program & Policy Booklet)
   *If a holiday falls on a weekend, I would take the Friday before. That way you are not losing a paid holiday off.

3) **Two weeks sick time off (PTO)** can be used for illness, funerals, etc.)
   I rarely used this time off. I am working from home, so unless I am really ill, I can muster through the day so as not to interrupt their work schedules. However, I would always send a text message to parents letting them know what I am dealing with, whether I or one of my own children are sick so they can determine if they want to bring their child but letting them know I am not closed. So, if they choose not to come to daycare, that is NOT counted as a day off for me against my number of days. I believe the only time I closed for a week and used my sick time was when each of my parents passed away and I needed to fly home to MN. Once for two days due to the Flu. Three times in 21 years is not a lot.

   Also, it's important to note, if you are open any more than 8 hours, and you should decide on a certain day that you will be closing at 3 p.m., this is NOT counted against your vacation days. You were open 8 hours of the 10½ hours you usually are. I only did this, for example, for a doctor appointment or if my kids had something going on, I had to be there for.

4) **Daycare closed December 24 - January 1 (Paid)**

You may feel this is a lot of time off. It is a reasonable time as offered by most businesses to their employees. You are your *own* boss. You make the rules, but they must be reasonable.

If after 10 years you want to add a couple of days of paid-time-off or even a week, you can if you feel there won't be much backlash. Any time you make a change to your daycare rules, descriptions, etc. you must inform your families with an updated Program & Policies. Highlighting the change so they don't have to try and find it.

I never increased mine from the above list, even after 21 years. I felt my time off was enough for me and sometimes just taking a long weekend is a great break as well.

Working with Families on Vacations

Because I tried to work my break time around my daycare families, I would ask them to give me their vacation schedules and I would pick the week when most were gone. That was almost always the week of July 4th.

My brother would fly down to SC and spend the week with my family on July 4th. Because anyone over the age of 15 must have a background check done to be around your children in daycare, it worked out well to have friends and family visit when I was going to be closed.

In my later years, I had two neighbors who had a background check done and went to a class to be allowed to be around the daycare kids. They were friends and would come over to hang in my pool. They also were backup for me if I needed one, so I didn't have to close my daycare for an hour doctor or dentist appointment for example. Parents always appreciated this so they wouldn't have to find alternate care that day simply for a 1-hour appointment. It's nice to have trustworthy people who are available for back-up.

Religion in Daycare

This is an important topic to bring up in an interview. Since I am Christian, I made it clear that not only do we recognize Santa and the Easter Bunny, but we also recognize The Nativity, Jesus, and the meaning of Easter. I also have some children's books on subjects like Noah, and Jesus' birth. I put up a Christmas tree for the kids to decorate in the playroom as well as a couple throughout my house of my own. I also let them know we have a Halloween party with costumes and games. I had one family who disagreed with Halloween and simply didn't come to daycare that day.

> **STORYTIME!**
> In all my years of daycare, I did find a family who didn't want their child exposed to a Christian atmosphere. They left my daycare just before Christmas, as I was having a Christmas Play regarding the Nativity Scene, in complete costume for our end of year party. That same family went to a couple of other daycares and eventually came back to mine. They told me they couldn't find one they were happy with and the kids were so happy at my daycare they wanted to come back, and I welcomed them back immediately.

If a family has a faith, they would like celebrated, such as the Jewish faith, possibly suggest they come to daycare one day as a guest and maybe read a child's story and explain it to the children.

Just be upfront with your families at the interview, so there are no surprises, and they can decide if your daycare is the right one for their family.

Chapter 19: Maternity Leave

You need a plan for when one of your families is expecting another baby while they have one in your care.

Their leave could be 6 weeks (typical) or it could be 3 months (typical for a C-Section birth). Some may even have stored up time off to have a longer break. So, you need a plan as to how you will handle them gone during this time. Do you want them to come back? This could be a time to sever ties if this family has been an issue. Or it's a time to be sure they understand your policies. You can't keep a place for them and receive no income from them.

Scenario: They have a child in your care. They plan to keep that child in daycare so mom can concentrate on the baby. So, she continues to pay as usual. Remember though, she needs to pay a deposit for the new baby that will be joining your daycare to hold her spot for the baby. A new file is made for the baby with all forms needed. But... What if she wants her child to come part-time? Or stay home with her while she is home with the baby? I have this broken down in my template for you to use on the Program and Policy booklet, which shows how it works. But let's give you some info here as well.

She has the child in your care stay at home with her during maternity leave:
- She needs to pay ½ of her regular week's rate to *keep* her spot.
- Should she want to bring her child one half of the time, that would be okay on the days that the *two of you* agree upon.
- You may find you can't afford to only accept ½ pay during this time. If that is the case, then a conversation needs to take place. If they want to stay and can afford it themselves, they will pay the full rate to keep their spot.

She wants to take longer than 6 weeks for maternity leave and keep the older child home.
- She needs to pay ½ rate for the older child to keep spot and then she needs to pay the full rate for that same child that started with week 7.
- She will need to pay either a full rate for the baby or ½ rate for the baby to keep the spot. That is something you will need to decide.

**If you don't have a plan and a signed contract of the arrangement, they could bail on you after a few weeks, and you are out the money and have to find a family now to take the spot that you have been holding for weeks! Possibly months!

STORYTIME!

I had a woman interview with me when she was 8 weeks pregnant. She had to pay me a two-week deposit for her baby for me to hold her spot and we had an agreed date when she would begin. If she didn't begin on that date due to the baby not coming on the expected date, she still needed to begin paying as if the baby was in my care. I have held that spot, therefore it is time to pay. Her baby wouldn't be coming for approximately 9 months, so any family I brought into my daycare, I had to keep in mind, I had a baby that would be starting in 9 months, and I had to have a spot open for that baby.

It is a risk. Holding a spot. Even with a two-week deposit. They could decide they are not coming after all, forfeit the deposit, but you could have possibly filled that spot long before and had the weekly income.

The reason I did this with this family, is she came recommended by my daughter's kindergarten teacher. She was also a kindergarten teacher who had an adjoining classroom with my daughter's classroom. Since I had volunteered there one day a week, I knew who she was. Plus, she was just so nice and so thorough. This is one of those families I became friends with and did things socially with. I loved their son, he was such a good baby and so beautiful. Sometimes she would hang out in the summertime, waiting for all the kids to leave and we would have margaritas poolside while our kids played in the pool. We are still friending all these years later.

Chapter 20: Taxes

You are running a self-employed business. I strongly suggest you contact an accountant who specializes in Daycares for your filings. There are many advantages to Daycare that may not be found by someone not familiar with it. Keep all receipts, record everything!

Create a spreadsheet with at least the following:

- Food Expense
- Travel miles (such as going to grocery stores, stores for supplies, field trips)
- Paper products
- Cleaning products
- Repair and maintenance expenses
- Entertainment
- Memberships for field trips
- Admission fees
- Gifts
- Toys
- Supplies
- Depreciation items (stereos, tv's playground equipment, etc.)
- Helper Fees
- Decorations
- Education materials
- Preschool Programs
- Party supplies
- Office expenses (paper, ink, etc.)
- Household items (light bulbs, batteries, water hoses, sprinklers)
- Basically, everything and anything you spend money on. It all has a percentage of discount for your taxes.

Whether you buy a new hose for the lawn or a lawnmower, these are things you can take a claim on. It is necessary to cut the lawn, or to water it and the flowers. Fertilizer, cookware, lamps... the list is endless.

Also, keep records of everything you did or cost you to set up your business. Did you fence your yard? Did you build a playset or buy one? Did you buy toys, storage bins, office supplies? Even at a garage sale, you may need to have a receipt book for sellers to sign. You simply need to put it in some order for your records. You need to know how much you have spent so you know what you have made.

Be sure to donate to thrift stores, humane societies, and/or charities. You will get a blank receipt with a date on it and stamped. Anything under $750 in some state will not require you to provide itemized receipts. My accountant gave me some grief as I was 'giving' my children's clothes to my nieces'. She said I should be donating to places that will give me a receipt to record on my taxes as charity. I still gave the clothes but also did the charities, etc.

There will be a **sample form** you can make for your tax accountant at the end of this book. I was with my accountant for so many years, I didn't need to send receipts. I simply had it all typed up for her. My expenses, losses, income, etc. In fact, when I moved to SC, I kept my accountant who was in MN because she was so good and knew all the ins and outs of doing daycare taxes. If she had a question, she would send me an email asking for example, "what is York Co Paws for Cause"? It was a thrift shop I donated things that helped the animals in the shelters and it's a tax write-off. You do need to keep **all** receipts and keep accurate records in case of an audit.

Hours

You also need to keep track of hours of operations. This includes but is not limited to your daycare hours of operation. You spend time shopping for food and supplies. You spend time interviewing, cooking for the next day sometimes, baking cookies for birthday parties. You spend time setting up your new playset, preparing materials for your next day of preschool or a craft. You purchased tomato plants to plant with the children for a gift for their dad. Everything is calculated, your time costs money, this is for your benefit.

You will be surprised at how many different things you need to buy, clean, shop, etc. to make your business work smoothly. Even time spent recording the above counts as 'time spent'. Your accountant will take a percentage of what was spent or depreciated on an item and by the time you are done, you will have a bottom line of taxable income. It will be much less after all calculations are complete. Remember the keywords here are 'taxable income'. When you run your own business, loss and expense are expected. Your accountant will also ask what rooms are used for your daycare.

I had a 4-bedroom home with 3 baths. I used all the rooms with the exception of my master bath. Depending on how many kids I had, sometimes the bedrooms were used for nap time, or if I had an infant or young one, I may have a crib in a couple of bedrooms. Even my dining room was used for laying out of projects that would go home with the kids along with their bags. Your accountant will take a percentage of this square footage as well for their calculations for your expenses.

One year I put my back out and I had to go to the hospital. A friend of mine who ran a daycare took my kids into hers while I was out. I had to pay her what I would have made that week. That was a loss of income and was recorded on my taxes. *Note: an example tax form is included with Forms at the back of this book.*

You will want to be sure to let parents know that you file taxes. I do this at the interview. You want them to know nothing is 'under the table' I would tell them, "though I look great in orange, I have no desire to wear it every day!" Lol.

You will submit a Tax Sheet to each family by the end of January of each year. This will show a total of all Daycare Payments, and any deposits paid in that tax year as well. Some companies have a 125 Form. Teachers usually have this form, for pre-tax dollars for daycare. I would fill those out if they brought that to me. You will show the family's name, the child's name, and the total amount paid that tax year. You will include your License/Register No., Your address, Name of business and you will sign it. I suggest though you will most likely have this on your computer, I stored a copy in their file as well.

Chapter 21: Your Own Kids in Daycare

Last but not least... having your own kids in your daycare can be wonderful! It was for me. My kids grew up with other daycare kids and made many friends through the years. They became so close that some of the kids would spend the night or go on camping trips with our family. And of course, you get to spend time with your own children. That's one of the reasons many people decide to start a daycare!

When my kids were ill, I didn't have to call my boss to say I won't be in today and hear that tone in the voice on the phone guilting me for not coming in. I was able to be there for my kids, watch them grow, learn, and interact with other kids. I could help with sharing not only their toys but also their mom.

However, it is very important that your children have their own space! A place that is not part of the daycare. I had my kids keep toys that were special to them in their bedrooms. They should always feel like they have some privacy or boundaries with others playing with their things. Their bedrooms were off-limits for playtime by daycare kids. I explained to my kids, if it's in the playroom, the daycare kids can play with it.

When my daughters were getting older, they became helpers, legally. I could claim them as such on my taxes. There is a set amount one can claim, plus bonuses they get throughout the year. Aside from the tax benefit, they helped me set up lunch, put bibs on young children, and even help to feed them. They played with the kids, grabbed diapers or bottles for me. They helped watch them on the playground or in our playroom. I knew my daughters would be good babysitters when they grew older and they would come with a lot of experience! I also knew they would be great parents, as they have seen and experienced all the different personalities of the kids through the years.

Doing Daycare as a career choice can be a great source of income! Daycare chose me. I was reluctant but I am so glad I did. It was the best choice for my family and for me as a mom. I hope you will feel the same way as well.

Needing Adult Interaction

I can't stress this enough! You are spending your days with children 5 days a week. If you have children, you also spend your nights with children 7 days a week. You need time for you. Time for conversations that are spent with adults. You need balance or you will burn out. Often, during nap times, I would call a girlfriend or my mom when she was still with us and talk. We would share, laugh, and sometimes address serious issues. It was a rejuvenating time, and it was needed.

Be sure to make time outside of daycare with your partner, your girlfriends, your extended family members. Go to lunch, go shopping, go to an event, anything that involves you and other adults. Yes, you will have interaction with parents at pick-up time that can involve some conversation, but you are still on the clock, you are still scanning the kids as they play and really it will only be for a short while that you have this interaction.   Which brings me to my last two STORY TIMES!

STORYTIME!

I was out for dinner with my teenage daughters. This was always something special and fun, as at this point in my life I am divorced and raising my daughters who are very busy with school and marching band. To have their attention and time was important to our family time. So, we went to the local restaurant for dinner and after we had ordered, I saw one of my daycare families at a large table with many adult friends and adult family members but also my little daycare child, I will call SuzieQ. SuzieQ sees me and comes running over to say hi to Ms. Tam. I hugged her and said hello and looked over to mom and dad letting them know I am aware they know she is over at my table. However, she wasn't there to just say hi. She climbed up into the empty chair and decided she was going to spend her time with me, giving her parents time to be adults. As she took over the conversation as she was quite the talker and a little more grown up for her age, my daughters and I were not getting our time together. Her parents made no attempt to have her come back to their table.

When this happened a few weeks later, same situation, crazy I know, but this was a local restaurant, and we loved their food, and it was close to home. This time when SuzieQ came to our table as her parents smiled at me, I said "Hello SuzieQ! So nice you are out with your family! Ms. Tam is out with her family too! Now you go back to your table and say hi to mom and dad for me" and she skipped off. Though we ran into them at other places, the situation of having her spend her time with me didn't happen again.

STORYTIME!

BEACH TRIP: Because we lived only 3.5 hours from Myrtle Beach, this is a popular place to take vacation time. My good friend Peggy and her boys (her boys are the same age as my girls, teens) were all planning a trip. Her boys were also in the marching band and we did a lot of things together. We were so excited for this long weekend we had planned. Sharing a condo on the beach, having crab and drinks and beach time! One of my daycare families (Suzie Q's) was planning a trip to the beach the same weekend with another of my daycare families because they were friends and so were their daughters. Suzie's mom asked where we were staying, and I told her. The next day, she announced they were staying at the same place and we could all hang out together. Her daughter and the other child were 4 years old. I couldn't believe it. My mini vacation was being hijacked. When I am on my own time, I am not Ms. Tam. I am Tamara or Mom, period. I love kids, don't get me wrong, but I don't want to hear "Ms. Tam watch me!" or "look at me!"

I have a friend who we get on really well and always have fun, as do our kids. I told her about it, and she said "absolutely not! This needs to be addressed". I agreed and because this is a delicate situation, and I don't want to offend or lose my daycare families over this, I needed to be careful. The other mom was someone I knew wouldn't take offense at what I was going to say and could maybe help me out. I contacted her and explained the following: I told her how excited I was for my mini-vacation and who I was going with. I explained that Suzie Q's mom was planning for them to join us. Spending time together would be fine if it was the original plan, but I felt it would be like taking my 'work' with me. I compared that when they go, they are leaving the office behind, the laptop behind, the boss behind. If they join us, my work is coming with me. I even explained about not being Ms. Tam while I am at the beach.

> She totally understood and said it was no big deal. She said she would tell Suzie's mom that they do the beach a lot and that she would like to do something different and would suggest they go to the Great Wolf Lodge that has an indoor waterpark. She also said she wouldn't divulge my feelings or that we even talked. I was so relieved and there were no hurt feelings. Whew! You need to protect your personal time.

Chapter 22: Making a Difference

Often you will find little moments or milestones in your career in Daycare that make you realize you are making a difference. The following are some stories that did that for me and for the child and their families.

RACHEL

She was a beautiful little girl with long dark hair and big brown eyes and a smile that could melt anyone's heart. She was 4 years old and her daycare had been cited for not being licensed and for having approximately 16-20 kids in their care.

I realized the first day that Rachel didn't know her colors, her numbers, her ABC's, or how to spell her own name. It wasn't because she lacked the ability but that she hadn't been taught these.

I asked her mom if I could work on all of these and said with her help, we could bring her up to speed by the end of the month as she would soon be tested for kindergarten for the following school year. When I was starting kindergarten, all they needed to know was how to tie their shoes, know the ABCs, be able to take care of your own bathroom duties, and count to ten.

Mom was on board. I had large colored cutouts that looked like large crayons. If it was a green one, then I had GREEN written on it and so on. I had cutouts for letters and numbers as well. All were laminated, actually given to me from one of my daycare moms who was a kindergarten teacher.

I would work with Rachel every day, along with the other kids and by Friday I would send her home with a large envelope of the ones she needed to work on, and they would come back on Monday. We worked with a Mega-Doodle (a modern-day etch-a-sketch) when working on writing her name. She loved doing this as she could erase easily with the slide and start again. We talked about upper-case and lower-case letters and that her name started with an upper-case and the rest were lower-case.

By week three she only had a couple of each group in her envelope and she could write her name proudly! Her mom was so thrilled and saw such a difference in Rachel with her new confidence and knowledge. By week four, her envelope was empty.

TJ

A very distraught mom called and asked if she could come interview for daycare. She arrived with this round face little boy with big brown eyes and blond hair with a flat top haircut. He was on the round side but not overweight. He was adorable. She was very honest immediately and said he had been terminated from the church daycare he was in, and another one before that as well for not listening and playing too rough.

She didn't know what to do, as she worked from home on the other side of our neighborhood but needed to be online and couldn't entertain him while she worked. After a long talk about how I run my daycare and talking with TJ, I told him, "I felt he was going to be a great new addition to our daycare and he would have lots of friends here and things would be okay, I just knew it." His mom was hesitant but encouraged.

TJ started the next day. I welcomed him and so did the kids who were already there. I showed him where he would put his things and told him we would be swimming soon in my pool and told him where to place his towel and suit. He was all smiles. I have to be honest; I didn't see much of an issue with TJ. When he would get a bit rambunctious, I would remind him we don't play like that. I talked to him. I asked him what makes him happy, what makes him laugh. He got lots of hugs and attention. We all were working on table manners and I told the kids that if they could use their manners out to eat and at home, they would get more trips to restaurants such as McDonald's. I even placed mirrors in front of some who couldn't grasp the idea of closing their mouths as they ate. It worked. They were rewarded with a trip to McDonald's and to play on the slides there if they ate their food and behaved as expected.

Two weeks later, the grandma came to pick up with TJ's mom and said she "couldn't believe the difference in his behavior!" She explained how she couldn't even take him out as he would run around like a maniac. She told me how TJ was respectful and behaved when she took him out and wanted to thank me for helping TJ so she could enjoy this beautiful grandson. I told her my feelings were simple-- he wasn't getting guidance at the daycares and he wasn't listened to. He wasn't given affection or attention and he was getting it here.

Fast forward ten years later. My daughter came to me and told me that there were two guys on bikes in the driveway that asked to see me. I saw the boys and asked "hey guys! What can I do for you?" Both boys appeared to be about 14 years old and had dark hair and were out for a bike ride. One of the boys said, "Don't you recognize me, Ms. Tam?" I looked closer and said "James?" (I had taken care of him at least ten years earlier before his parents split up and his mom moved out of the neighborhood) and as I looked at the other boy, I said "TJ? Oh my God! Look at you!" He was slim and dark-haired now and his round face was gone and replaced with that of a strapping young teen. They said they were riding past my house and wanted to stop and say hi. My heart just melted. We chatted a few minutes and when they left, I felt a sense of accomplishment. They were mature and well-mannered and respectful, and I knew I had a hand in that, and they remembered me and cared enough to stop and say hi, which made me feel so good.

Note from the Author:

If you find that in starting your Daycare business you have found things not included in this Guide, please contact me at tamarahessler@hotmail.com to set up a Zoom appointment for a fee. As I am well aware, some unique situations arise that just don't fit into a black or white area. I'd love to help you in your personal experience to act as that "next-door neighbor Daycare provider" for you!

Below are the templates and forms I have used in my Daycare over the years. Feel free to personalize them.

Thanks again for reading and I wish you well in your new adventure and business!

Sincerely,

Miss Tam

CHECKLIST: SETTING UP THE HOME

1. Gates for stairways up and down.
2. Gates for utility areas if the door can't be closed.
3. Deadbolt on doors to outside (leading to pool/street/etc.).
4. Cover all outlets with safety tabs.
5. Make-up storm drill with a blueprint of the home of where you and children will go (can be hand-drawn) and displayed (can be on the inside of a front closet door for the Fire Marshall or DSS to see.
6. Make up a Fire Drill plan with where the 'meeting place' will be outside the home should anyone become separated.
7. Close the back of wooden stairs from decks, etc.
8. All cleaning items stored either in cabinets up high or childproof locks on the cabinet doors.
9. If you have a gas stove with knobs on the front just above the oven door, they need to be removed during daycare hours (when not in use).
10. The water heater cannot be set hotter than 120 degrees Fahrenheit
11. 3-6 bottles of Ipecac (to induce vomiting in case of poisoning).
12. Files on each animal/pet with their medical records and licensing information.
13. Install self-latching handles on gates to play areas (to keep kids from going out to the street or pool if there is one).
14. All cords on blinds must be out of reach.
15. Set up an appointment with Fire Marshall once all is done.
16. Apply for a business license and pay the fee with the City.

CHECKLIST: PLAYROOM

(This is a suggestion list to use for the most part)

1. Shelving (no tall shelving unless bolted to the wall)
2. Storing bins for toys
3. Plastic Drawers on Wheels
4. Sleeping Mats
5. Bins for kids' blankets/pillows
6. Age-appropriate games/toys
7. Baby/toddler toys
8. Approved crib/s (keep paperwork for proof)
9. Pack N Play for only playing in, for a young child, not for napping.
10. Books including board books for young children.
11. Puzzles, age-appropriate
12. Legos/Blocks
13. Cars/trucks
14. Baby dolls/baby doll blankets/baby bottles
15. Strollers for dolls/highchairs for dolls
16. Kitchen Set/dishes/pretend food/utensils
17. Child size table and chairs or picnic-style table
18. Posters or Pictures on walls for decoration or educational
19. TV for age-appropriate programs/movies
20. Musical items such as drums, tambourine, bells, guitar (stay away from things like recorders/flutes that require the mouth to play with)
21. Blankets for building forts

CHECKLIST: FOR OUTSIDE PLAYGROUND

1. Wooden Playset (many cities/neighborhoods do not allow the metal kind) with swings, slides, etc.
2. Sandbox but only the kind with a cover (keeps pests out)
3. Large and small bouncy balls
4. Picnic table
5. Cars/trucks
6. Plastic Playhouse
7. Avoid trampolines, many insurance companies will not cover your house, etc. if you have one.
8. Water table
9. Pools (check with your local DSS if they allow any kind of pool, including baby pools)
10. Sprinklers can be a source of fun if pools are not allowed.
11. Water guns
12. Freestanding teeter-totter
13. Some playsets have a teeter-totter style that can be attached. I removed the monkey rings and had one installed and a robe swing that had a disk to sit on.

CHECKLIST: FOR OUTSIDE TOYS

(typically used in driveways or empty garages, patios)

1. Riding Toys
2. Skateboards
3. Basketball hoop regular size
4. Basketball hoop child size
5. Bucket of Chalk
6. Balls (but you may need to park a vehicle at the end of the driveway to stop balls from going in the street)
7. Yellow Caution Sign (I put one next to my van at the end of the driveway for passing cars). Walmart, Target, etc. sells them.
8. Scooters

Typically, you need enough toys for all kids to have something to play with. If you have 6 kids that doesn't mean you need 6 riding toys, but you should have several and they can take turns.

SUPPLIES NEEDED FOR EVERYDAY

1. Baby changing pad that can be washed off.
2. Spray bottle with bleach and water/disinfectant wipes for pad
3. Latex gloves for changing baby diapers
4. An extra box of wet wipes
5. Extra diapers (if the parent forgets to bring)
    a. I would take an extra diaper from the daily bag over a few days, so I would have an extra stash for days when it's needed.
6. Clorox Wipes for counters
7. Soap with pump and paper towels for drying hands. No bar soap.
8. Highchairs and or boosters for mealtime
9. Boxes of tissues
10. Disinfectant spray

SUPPLIES TO BE BROUGHT BY FAMILIES

1. Sunscreen Spray (no lotions) & Sunscreen stick for face
2. Wet Wipes
3. Diapers
4. Pull-ups
5. Butt Cream (for rashes, don't assume what you may have can be used for that child)
6. Extra pair of clothes to be kept in the bag
7. Hairbrush or hair ties to be kept in the bag
8. Extra pair of underwear and socks to be kept in the bag
9. Teething gel to be kept in the bag
10. Tylenol to be kept in the bag with instructions by the parent
11. Bathing suit/trunks for water play (can be kept at daycare)
12. Sun hat (especially for light-haired children)

Program and Policies Form
[*insert name*] Daycare Program and Policies

[Your name, address, City, State, Zip, and Lic./Reg. #]

***Goal*:** Is to provide a safe, clean, and fun environment for your children and mine. I am aware of how important it is to you and your children that we work together to provide the most stable and comfortable place for them to grow and develop physically, mentally, and spiritually and to provide a healthy environment such as a smoke-free environment.

Program: My program will be flexible depending on the time of year, weather, and just the day. Most days will include some or all of the following:

- Play-time: choices of play materials such as dolls, cars/trucks, puzzles, markers, crayons, paper, games, blocks, dress-up clothes, paints, and other options. Clean-up time.
- Lunch and a nutritional snack depending on your hours.
- Stories, art projects, large muscle activities, songs, and dance.
  - **Preschool - arts/crafts/*learning Program for 2 1/2 & over (*during the Sept. - May School year).**
- Rest time for those under 4 from approx. 1 p.m. to 3 p.m. and quiet time for everyone else at this time. Reading is encouraged for school-age kids for the first 30 minutes of quiet time.
- Outside time if weather and time permits.
- Final clean-up time.

Possible outings such as parks, picnics, beaches, etc. If an admission fee is required, such as the Zoo or Children's museum, etc., you will be responsible for that and you will be notified in advance. Children will be properly restrained in the vehicle at all times. I have brightly colored shirts with "Tam's Kids" on them that I usually have the children wear depending on the outing.

Information about me: [This is a Bio of you and your family]

Days and hours of service: I will be open for daycare at 7 a.m. (only **if needed,** otherwise I will open at **8 a.m.** - 5 p.m.-ish. **Monday - Friday.** Each individual will discuss and agree upon your arrival and pick-up time, according to your **work** schedule. If your hours change for any reason, please discuss this with me to be sure the hours work out with my daycare hours. It is important for many reasons that you can always be reached in case of an emergency. If your workday ends early, I will plan for you to pick up early, however, if we have discussed this prior and it is agreed, please have an alternate phone number available for me. I request that if you have a cell phone, that I have that number for my records. Thank you for your cooperation.

Pick-up time: You must pick up on time. Weather and traffic, at times, can be a problem, however, please plan for delays and leave accordingly. I do not at this time charge a late fee, though I have in the past. I haven't had problems with parents picking up late and haven't had a need. I understand there are times when running personal errands may need to happen, just try to be considerate of me and let me know if you are running late, and for the sake of the child or children who are counting on their parents to be there on time. If your pickup time is during naptime, consideration for the other children, a quick and quiet pickup is much appreciated.

Drop-off time: If you are arriving when Daycare first opens in the morning please <u>do not come earlier</u>. I will turn my outside lights on and unlock my front door when daycare is open. If you are not coming for daycare, regardless of your drop-off time, please call me ahead of time so that I can plan accordingly. Without a call, I am expecting you and have prepared for your arrival. If you are calling the evening before, please do not call after 10:00 p.m. If you are calling in the morning, no earlier than 6:30 a.m., please. Also please know if you don't show for daycare within 15 minutes of your drop off time, I will call. Many times, we hear of children left in vehicles when mom or dad are on autopilot and the child is left in a hot or cold car. I have always thought *"if only the daycare provider had called."*

Also, please just walk in when arriving for Daycare. You do not need to knock or ring the bell. I am expecting you, so this is not a problem. **Reader: (NOTE; This may or may not work for you. I didn't want to have to go to the door if I was busy with a child or have my dog bark from the doorbell).**

Quick drop-offs are appreciated, as the longer you stay, the chance the child feels he or she can go with you. It creates upset children for both those arriving and those witnessing the upset. Usually, children are excited to come to daycare, and the longer you stay they start to question what they are doing, staying or going with mom or dad. Also, I am trying to get my day going with the kids and prolonged goodbyes make that difficult. Rarely does a child complain or cry once mom or dad leave, so quick departures are good for everyone. If your child would for any reason not be able to settle, I would call you immediately.

You may always come early to pick up your child or children, however, for the safety of the children and me, my door may be locked. I can supply you the code to my garage door and you can always enter through there if my door is locked. I believe parents should <u>always feel free to "show up" anytime.</u> If you need to pick up early, (during the scheduled nap times) a call would be appreciated so that I may open my door It would also help if you do plan to pick a small child up early (that is a napper) to let me know so that I can have them nap in a separate room than the others, so I don't disturb their naps while retrieving your child. I will try to have the doors unlocked at the end of each day when you are picking up and I can monitor the door. During the warmer months, when the children may be playing outside, I ask that you <u>park in the street if children are in the driveway</u> playing games such as basketball, or jump rope, for the safety of the children.

Cell Phone: I carry a phone with me at all times when away from home. If for any reason you need to reach me, you may call me at _____.

Paid Holidays and vacation time: I will not be open for daycare on the following days. Please make other arrangements if you are required to work holidays. There will be a regular charge if this holiday falls on one of your regularly scheduled daycare days. If a paid holiday falls on a weekend, I will receive the day closest to that (either side of the weekend)) as my paid holiday. However, I usually take Fri.

Labor Day	**Good Friday**	**Easter Monday**	**Memorial Day**
July 4th	**Christmas Eve**	**Christmas Day**	**New Year's Eve**
New Year's Day & Jan 2nd	**MLK**	**Thanksgiving Thurs./Friday**	

I will be closed and paid for any and all weekdays between Christmas Eve and January 2nd with two additional weeks to be used at another time during the calendar year.

I will receive 10 personal paid days a year from January through December that I can use as sick days for me or my children or any other reason I may need a day off. These days will not accumulate if I do not use them during the calendar year. If our family should decide to vacation any time other than the listed holidays or personal/vacation days. That time will be unpaid to me and you will receive as much notice as possible.

Maternity Leave: You may take 6 weeks maternity leave, however, to <u>keep</u> your placement of a child already in my care, you will need to pay 1/2 of your normal weekly rate during the 6-week period. (This is assuming your older child is home with you during your maternity leave) Your child may also come for 1/2 of the days normally here, on days that we both agree on. If you choose to take maternity leave for longer than 6 weeks, you will need to begin paying your full week payment whether your child returns or not during that period, along with the added full rate of the infant. This is to hold your placement here in my daycare for the older child as well as your infant.

Summer Schedules: Sometimes I have parents with different schedules in the summer, such as Teachers. I have a 3-day minimum per week regarding my rates. Please talk to me so we can make arrangements for your child to have a placement in my daycare. Please don't assume I will have room if you haven't discussed this with me. It has been common for my daycare to have older siblings not normally here in the summertime. Also, if you are not here in the summertime, the only way to ensure you have a placement in the Fall is to pay throughout the summer months either prepaid or every Monday, I will accept a 3-day min/week for the summer months if you want to ensure placement. You may also bring your child for those 3 days a week or less if you should need a day to yourself. That has been nice not only for you but for the child to remain in contact with me and his or her playmates. If you choose not to pay for the summer while you are not working, I will always try to have a place for your child.

Payment: I will be paid weekly on Monday <u>morning</u>, no later than noon, for that week of childcare whether your week begins on Monday or not. There will be a $15.00 Service Fee for any late checks. If a check is returned, you will be responsible for the $15.00

Service Fee and any charges incurred from the bank at which time *only* cash payment will be accepted. Placing your check payment in your child's backpack or Friday Folder on Sunday night usually eliminates forgetting. Please know if any late fees aren't included in your next weeks' check, it will be deducted from your deposit. You have the option to pay the previous Friday. Please plan on paying the previous Friday if a paid holiday falls on Monday, and Daycare is closed, or if you are not coming for Daycare on Monday. This will eliminate me having to call you.

Meals/Snacks: *Meals will be served at the following times.*
Lunch: I usually feed my toddlers and preschoolers around 11:30 a.m. Naps begin at approximately 12:30 p.m. depending on what that morning activity has been.
Afternoon Snack: Between 3-3:30 p.m. or when **all** are up from naps.

Forms: *I must have the following forms signed and dated by parents before the first day of care in my home:*
- **Contract aka Admissions form**
- **Copy of your child's immunizations**
- **Swimming Permission form**
- **Photo permission form**
    These forms included in the back of the book
- *Monitor/Nap Form (for those younger than 4 years)***
- *Outside Play for 4 years old and up***
    **I previously had forms for these 2 things, however, states are making their own determinations of whether or not that is allowed anymore.

Pets: [Tell them about your pets, ages, names, and how they are with the kids and that they are up to date on all shots.]

Sick Children: *Before illness strikes, PLAN AHEAD.* You will need to arrange back-up daycare if you cannot stay home with sick children, or if I am ill. There will be a regular fee for these days. If your child is not here regularly, Monday through Friday, do not assume you can use other days as your days in daycare. I may have an activity planned for the expected number of children or a field trip planned with a certain number of children planned for the available seats available in my van.

Your child will not be accepted here for daycare if he/she has:
- Temperature - 100 degrees (underarm or ear)
- Conjunctivitis - an eye infection commonly referred to as "Pink Eye".
- Bronchitis - which can begin with hoarseness, cough, and a slight elevation in temperature, the cough may be dry and painful, but it gradually becomes productive.
- Rashes - that you cannot identify or have not been diagnosed by a doctor.
- Head lice.
- Flu - keep home **24 hours after symptoms end**.
    - A. Diarrhea   B. Vomiting
- <u>Severe</u> cold.
- Strep Throat - or other illnesses treated with an antibiotic. Your child should not be brought to daycare until he/she has been on the medication for <u>at least 24 hours</u>.
- If your child becomes sick without obvious symptoms or is unusually and extremely distressed and can't be consoled.
- Specific <u>contagious</u> diseases/illnesses - measles, chickenpox, mumps, etc.
- Pneumonia.

It is my responsibility to do everything possible to prevent contagious infections from spreading to the other children, including my children and myself. If your child develops an illness while in my care, he/she will be separated from the other children and you will be called to pick up your child immediately. If you have more than one child in my care, please be prepared to pick up your children. If one is ill, *they* must stay home. **This is to help stop the spread of an illness that a sibling has had more contact with** and to alleviate upset children being left behind. Children always do better at home when ill and recover quicker. Please let me know as soon as possible if your child develops an infectious condition. If you find a need to give your child medication because of <u>severe cough</u> or fever, etc. this is the reason to keep them home. **If your child is not up to participating in normal activities or outings, this too is a reason to keep your child home until they are well.** I am not in a position to determine why a child may have any of the above symptoms. If you feel it is due to an allergy, you will need to have that determined by a physician and you may not have your child return to daycare until the symptoms are gone. When called to pick up your child due to illness, be prepared to have them stay at home the following day <u>and</u> allow for 24 hours after symptoms <u>end</u> before returning to daycare.

Please understand if a call to you is necessary, I have already determined your child must be picked up <u>unless stated otherwise</u>. If it is determined your child will be picked up and I ask you to call me regarding your child's recovery, please do so before coming back to daycare to eliminate any confusion whether your child will be accepted back yet. My daycare is known as a healthy daycare because I enforce rules regarding illness and that should make you feel better about your child's environment.

If <u>*my children*</u> are ill, I will call to inform you, only if I feel it is something you may not want your child in contact with. They are older and will be in a room away from your children and most likely will not be a problem for your child's health welfare. You may decide if you want to bring your child/children at that time. I will not close daycare unless they need constant care. I will inform you if that is the case. If you choose not to bring your child, there will **not** be any deduction in childcare expenses for that week. If I close my daycare, it will be considered a paid personal day.

Prescription medicines: I will not administer any prescription medicines that are not in the current original bottle with the child's name, doctor, and date printed. You may want to request that your pharmacist divide it into two bottles so I can keep one for your convenience. Then you won't need to worry about forgetting it at home or me forgetting to give it back at pick-up time.

Exception: *I use Orajel and Tylenol (provided by you) for teething pain.*

Items Needed:
- Extra set of clothes (to be kept here for toddlers)
- Swimwear and towel (summer) One bottle/can of sunscreen (min. #30 protection) to be kept here.
- Hairbrush (I do not allow the sharing of combs or hairbrushes)
- Please have your child wear a light jacket in case of cooler weather or outdoor play in the mornings.

Newsletter:

I will email this to you. At times you may receive more than one from me during the week. This would be because something came up that I need to make you aware of. Please read each and everyone, even if it appears that there is repetitive information (I sometimes keep some information in for several weeks to be sure everyone has received the information) I will scan in photos when I can but will also email cute photos taken of your child or children with the others here for your enjoyment and albums.

Nappers: Feel free to send a blanket to sleep with at naptime, or you may keep one here. I do not allow pacifiers in daycare for toddlers <u>while walking about</u>, however, <u>infants are the exception.</u>

If your toddler uses diapers, you will need to bring a bag of diapers and a BOX of wipes. I will let you know when I am running low. Also, if your child is in diapers, one-piece outfits or overalls are fine as long as they **have snaps in the bottom.** (If your child is potty training, please wear training friendly pants, such as elastic waist pants. Please avoid snap, button pants.) I will support that effort but ask that your child uses pull-ups until they are <u>completely</u> trained to avoid accidents on furniture and carpeting. How to know that a child who is potty trained: *My* definition is: When a child can completely take care of <u>all</u> tasks in the bathroom, i.e., pulling up/down of panties/underwear, cleaning oneself, and washing one's hands. I understand there are times when older children who are potty trained may need assistance and I will be happy to help them.

Children will need tennis shoes in summer, NO SANDALS WITH WORKING BUCKLES. I prefer Velcro or slip-on shoes to encourage self-help skills and for convenience.

Discipline: There may be times when a child is being disruptive or disrespectful of the other children or me. My first response will be to talk to the child about the behavior and how I would like for them to behave. If this is unsuccessful, a "time-out" is issued. This time is usually for 1-minute for each year they are, i.e., 4 years old = 4 minutes. Only if I am having difficulty with your child or if something has arisen that I feel you should be made aware of will I talk to you about your child's behavior. **Most situations that occur are normal and expected** occasionally. **I will not spank children**, please do not ask me to do so, even if this something you do in your home.

Bathroom/Eating Information: Only if your child has experienced something out of the ordinary will I discuss these issues. Exceptions: For Infants, I will inform you (verbally) of your child's consumption of formula or mother's milk, and the number of wet and or soiled diapers.

Toys/Food from home: It is up to you if you bring toys from home, however, please understand I cannot be responsible for those that come here with your children. It can cause problems for kids with sharing and lost or broken toys. I can't be responsible for your toys so please leave them at home or in the car unless your child is willing to share and understands I will put it up if they don't. I do not allow chewing gum or suckers in daycare. Please do not send food or treats of any kind with your child **unless** it is a special treat to be shared by all. If your child is eating something on the way here, please leave what may be left in the car.

Contract: A contract will be agreed upon and signed (by both of us) before your child starts at my home. Children will be accepted on a three-week trial basis. If arrangements are not mutually satisfactory, this contract may be terminated without notice. After the initial three weeks, care may be terminated with a one-week notice. In the event of a major discipline problem, daycare may be terminated without notice. A one-week prepaid deposit will be expected at the time contract is signed. **(This is used for the last week of daycare providing there is no immediate termination necessary.** In the case of a need for immediate termination, the deposit will **not** be returned. Payment is required for your child's care for the week beginning each **Monday.**

You will receive a Total of Daycare Payments for the year in January for your tax records. Your canceled check is your receipt for payments weekly. If you require a written receipt weekly, I will be happy to sign the receipt that will need to be supplied by you. I will also sign your 125k forms when needed.

I will not discriminate on the basis of race, color, national origin, religion, or sex.

Tamara J. Hessler

The policies read in this booklet may be revised at my discretion and will take precedence over any and all or previous or other contracts or admission forms. You may always request an updated Program & Policy Form.

This daycare home is non-smoking 24 hours a day and weapons-free home 24 hours a day. This is also a Christian Daycare, i.e., Christmas and Easter will be celebrated as such along with Santa and the Easter Bunny.

Updated _____
                Month, Date, Year

Admissions Contract Form

"Name of Daycare" Reg/License #_____
Owner/Operator: _____

Name of Child_____
Age _____ D.O.B._____
Address of Child_____

Any known allergies/food allergies_____
Name & No. Physician_____
Name & No. Dentist _____

If I cannot be reached in a case of emergency, _____ has my/our permission to contact my child's doctor/dentist: _____ Int.

Hours/Days Needed for Daycare _____

Deposit Paid $_____ Date Paid _____

Name of Mother/Guardian _____
Address_____
City/State_____
Email _____
Cell Phone _____
Mom's workplace_____
Name of Father/Guardian _____
Address _____
City/State_____

Email_____

Cell phone_____

Dad's workplace_____

Names of those allowed to pick up child/ren if parents do not
_____

I give permission for _____ to take photos of my child to be used for the Private Parent Facebook Page, for advertising of daycare openings. _____Initial

I understand that a full two-week deposit is to be paid before my child may begin daycare unless other arrangements have been made _____Initial.

My child has permission to be transported by _____ for field trips etc. in her vehicle with proper restraints. _____Initial.

My rate for daycare is determined by _____regarding the number of days, and hours needed. If the number of hours/days need to be changed by the parent, or by _____, a new contract will be drawn up and signed and if there is an increase in days, an added amount may be needed to cover the deposit requirements. If it decreases, there are no refunds given from the deposit as it is applied as stated in the Program and Policy when daycare is no longer needed. If there is a rate change it will be given with a minimum of three weeks' notice to the parent/guardian.

Daycare for my child will begin on _____

I have read and understand and agree to abide by the continued information in the Program and Policies listed in my hard copy or emailed to me and understand they may evolve over time and will be notified if there is a change.

_____Date_____
Parent/Guardian

All forms will be filled out as needed as they apply:
Please initial if completed:

Swimming Form _____
DSS Form _____
Immunization Form_____

Tamara J. Hessler

Swimming Permission Form

"your daycare name" Swimming Permission Form

I _____give permission for _____ to go in the swimming pool/wading pool located behind _____ home to swim, <u>providing she is present</u> at all times. If _____ needs to leave the area for any reason, all children will be removed from the pool until _____, or another adult returns to supervise the children.

#1 ___(int.) My child has had swimming instruction and/or knows how to swim.

#2_____(int.) My child will need to wear a life vest at all times when in the pool or playing near the pool because he/she does not know how to swim proficiently.

#3_____ (int.) I carry medical insurance and assume responsibility for allowing my child to swim in _____ pool/wading pool. I will not hold _____ liable for any injury.

#4_____(int.) My child does **not** have my permission to swim in the large swimming pool but may use the wading pool.

#5 _____(int.) I also understand that if I do not sign this permission form, my child will not be allowed in either pool but will be allowed to play in the fenced play area in the backyard while others may be swimming.

<u>**If #3 is not initialed, your child will not be allowed in either pool.**</u>

Date_____Signature_____
"name of daycare", "address of daycare" "city of daycare" "State of Daycare" "zip code of daycare" "phone number of daycare" "Registration/License Number of Daycare"

Tax Form for Daycare Families

_____DAYCARE
(Your daycare name)

_____
Your Name

_____
Your Address

_____
Your City, State, Zip Code

Registered Daycare Provider in the state of _____.
Tax ID # _____
Reg. # _____

Daycare Payments for _____ in the year: _____.
                      Child's name

Deposits paid (if any) paid in the year _____ in the amount of $_____

Parents: _____
                Parents names/name

Daycare Provider: _____
                         Daycare Provider's name

Daycare Provider's signature: _____

Date of signature: _____

Rates Template

(This is an example of estimated rates in Minneapolis, MN 2020, you may need to alter rates)

INFANTS (6 weeks – 12 months)
$190/week (5 Days)
$135/3 days
$45/drop in (1 day)

TODDLER (1 year – 3 years)
$181.00/week (5 days)
$120.00/3 days

PRESCHOOL (3 years – 5 years, not in kindergarten)
$171.00/week (5 days)
$114.00/3 days

SCHOOL AGE (5 years in kindergarten – 10 years)
(during summer or when school is out for vacation)
$150.00/week (5 days)
$105.00/3 days

SCHOOL AGE (during the school year)
Before School only: $60/week
After School only: $75/week includes snack
Before & After School: $90/week, includes after school snack

DROP-INS
- Take your 5-day weekly rate for age group divide by 5 and add at least $5 - $8 to the daily rate.
- The added amount to the average daily rate is because you are helping them with an immediate need, but also because it is disrupting your normal schedule to accommodate them.
- DEPOSITS: <u>Two weeks of daycare</u>.
    - Example: $190.00 a week, Deposit is: $380.00

A Note on Rates

You will get a feel for a family of their financial situation as you interview, such as where they work, their demeanor.

I have at times offered a sort of payment plan regarding the daycare deposit, as it's a lot to pay out initially.

They would be paying two weeks deposit, plus one-week daycare to begin.

In the above example that would be $570.00 to begin daycare!

I would tell them that they could split the deposit up, between anywhere from two to three weeks along with their weekly daycare payment.

Keep good records of weekly payments and what was weekly daycare payment and what was applied against the deposit.

File Information Request Form

Dear Parents,

Please forward the following information needed for your files on or before Daycare begins for your child/ren:

1. Your complete Name and Work Address, along with the phone number listed on your contract.
2. Address and Phone number of those allowed to pick up your child in case of emergency or a need on your contract.
3. An updated immunization from your child's physician to keep in their file.

You may send it to me via email or send it along in your child's bag.

Thank you.

_____ of _____ Daycare
    Your name   *Name of Daycare*

Legal Disclaimer

All forms, contracts, and templates are intended to be considered and modified for your use. Tamara Hessler is not responsible for any legal issues that may arise in the use of such forms, contracts, and templates. Any and all information contained within this book does not constitute legal advice.

Designations used by companies to distinguish their products are often claimed as trademarks. All brand names and product names used in this book and on its cover are trade names, service marks, trademarks, and registered trademarks of their respective owners. The publishers and the book are not associated with any product or vendor mentioned in this book. None of the companies referenced within the book have endorsed the book.

Tamara Hessler has no responsibility for the persistence or accuracy of URLs for external or third-party Internet Websites referred to in this publication and does not guarantee that any content on such Websites is, or will remain, accurate or appropriate.

Although the publisher and the author have made every effort to ensure that the information in this book was correct at press time and while this publication is designed to provide accurate information in regard to the subject matter covered, the publisher and the author assume no responsibility for errors, inaccuracies, omissions, or any other inconsistencies herein and hereby disclaim any liability to any party for any loss, damage, or disruption caused by errors or omissions, whether such errors or omissions result from negligence, accident, or any other cause.

This publication is meant as a source of valuable information for the reader, however, it is not meant as a substitute for direct expert assistance. If such a level of assistance is required, the services of a competent professional should be sought.

Tamara Hessler asserts the moral right to be identified as the author of this work.

All rights reserved. No part of this publication may be reproduced, stored, or transmitted in any form or by any means, electronic, mechanical, photocopying, recording, scanning, or otherwise without written permission from the publisher. It is illegal to copy this book, post it to a website, or distribute it by any other means without permission.

Acknowledgement

I didn't search out this field of daycare. It came to me, from a neighbor who was closing his down and wanted to be sure the children in his care had a place. I am thankful that he knocked on my door and planted the idea.

I am thankful to Kim Raberge. She was my neighbor at our new house, who had 13 years already under her belt as a daycare provider and became my mentor. She was awesome!

I am also thankful for the support of my family in this. As it does become a family affair. My daughters were very much a part of this career, as they were helpers, entertainers, swim coaches, craft helpers, especially when we did finger painting! Summers were awesome as they helped with so much since they weren't in school.

My daughter, Emily encouraged me to see this through. She acted as my Editor, along with research and legal support.

I could have made it work by myself, but with their help and support it made it so much easier and for that I am eternally grateful.

www.ingramcontent.com/pod-product-compliance
Lightning Source LLC
Chambersburg PA
CBHW081432220526
45466CB00008B/2356